Interactive Notebooks

Grade 7

Credits

Author: Katie Kee Daughtrey
Content Editors: Elise Craver, Christine Schwab, Angela Triplett

Visit *carsondellosa.com* for correlations to Common Core, state, national, and Canadian provincial standards.

Carson-Dellosa Publishing LLC
PO Box 35665
Greensboro, NC 27425 USA
carsondellosa.com

978-1-4838-3127-5
02-282177784

Table of Contents

The Number System

Ratios and Proportional Relationships

Expressions and Equations

Geometry

Statistics and Probability

Reproducibles

What Are Interactive Notebooks?

Interactive notebooks are a unique form of note taking. Teachers guide students through creating pages of notes on new topics. Instead of being in the traditional linear, handwritten format, notes are colorful and spread across the pages. Notes also often include drawings, diagrams, and 3-D elements to make the material understandable and relevant. Students are encouraged to complete their notebook pages in ways that make sense to them. With this personalization, no two pages are exactly the same.

Because of their creative nature, interactive notebooks allow students to be active participants in their own learning. Teachers can easily differentiate pages to address the levels and needs of each learner. The notebooks are arranged sequentially, and students can create tables of contents as they create pages, making it simple for students to use their notebooks for reference throughout the year. The interactive, easily personalized format makes interactive notebooks ideal for engaging students in learning new concepts.

Using interactive notebooks can take as much or as little time as you like. Students will initially take longer to create pages but will get faster as they become familiar with the process of creating pages. You may choose to only create a notebook page as a class at the beginning of each unit, or you may choose to create a new page for each topic within a unit. You can decide what works best for your students and schedule.

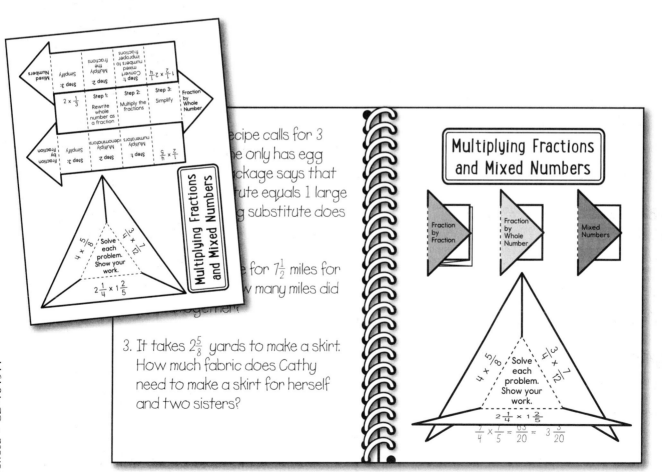

A student's interactive notebook for multiplying fractions and mixed numbers

Getting Started

You can start using interactive notebooks at any point in the school year. Use the following guidelines to help you get started in your classroom. (For more specific details, management ideas, and tips, see page 10.)

1. **Plan each notebook.**

   Use the planning template (page 9) to lay out a general plan for the topics you plan to cover in each notebook for the year.

2. **Choose a notebook type.**

   Interactive notebooks are usually either single-subject, spiral-bound notebooks, composition books, or three-ring binders with loose-leaf paper. Each type presents pros and cons. See page 5 for a more in-depth look at each type of notebook.

3. **Allow students to personalize their notebooks.**

   Have students decorate their notebook covers, as well as add their names and subjects. This provides a sense of ownership and emphasizes the personalized nature of the notebooks.

4. **Number the pages and create the table of contents.**

   Have students number the bottom outside corner of each page, front and back. When completing a new page, adding a table of contents entry will be easy. Have students title the first page of each notebook "Table of Contents." Have them leave several blank pages at the front of each notebook for the table of contents. Refer to your general plan for an idea of about how many entries students will be creating.

5. **Start creating pages.**

   Always begin a new page by adding an entry to the table of contents. Create the first notebook pages along with students to model proper format and expectations.

This book contains individual topics for you to introduce. Use the pages in the order that best fits your curriculum. You may also choose to alter the content presented to better match your school's curriculum. The provided lesson plans often do not instruct students to add color. Students should make their own choices about personalizing the content in ways that make sense to them. Encourage students to highlight and color the pages as they desire while creating them.

After introducing topics, you may choose to add more practice pages. Use the reproducibles (pages 78–96) to easily create new notebook pages for practice or to introduce topics not addressed in this book.

Use the grading rubric (page 11) to grade students' interactive notebooks at various points throughout the year. Provide students copies of the rubric to glue into their notebooks and refer to as they create pages.

What Type of Notebook Should I Use?

Spiral Notebook

The pages in this book are formatted for a standard one-subject notebook.

Pros

- Notebook can be folded in half.
- Page size is larger.
- It is inexpensive.
- It often comes with pockets for storing materials.

Cons

- Pages can easily fall out.
- Spirals can snag or become misshapen.
- Page count and size vary widely.
- It is not as durable as a binder.

Tips

- Encase the spiral in duct tape to make it more durable.
- Keep the notebooks in a central place to prevent them from getting damaged in desks.

Composition Notebook

Pros

- Pages don't easily fall out.
- Page size and page count are standard.
- It is inexpensive.

Cons

- Notebook cannot be folded in half.
- Page size is smaller.
- It is not as durable as a binder.

Tips

- Copy pages meant for standard-sized notebooks at 85 or 90 percent. Test to see which works better for your notebook.

Binder with Loose-Leaf Paper

Pros

- Pages can be easily added, moved, or removed.
- Pages can be removed individually for grading.
- You can add full-page printed handouts.
- It has durable covers.

Cons

- Pages can easily fall out.
- Pages aren't durable.
- It is more expensive than a notebook.
- Students can easily misplace or lose pages.
- Larger size makes it more difficult to store.

Tips

- Provide hole reinforcers for damaged pages.

How to Organize an Interactive Notebook

You may organize an interactive notebook in many different ways. You may choose to organize it by unit and work sequentially through the book. Or, you may choose to create different sections that you will revisit and add to throughout the year. Choose the format that works best for your students and subject.

An interactive notebook includes different types of pages in addition to the pages students create. Non-content pages you may want to add include the following:

Title Page

This page is useful for quickly identifying notebooks. It is especially helpful in classrooms that use multiple interactive notebooks for different subjects. Have students write the subject (such as "Math") on the title page of each interactive notebook. They should also include their full names. You may choose to have them include other information such as the teacher's name, classroom number, or class period.

Table of Contents

The table of contents is an integral part of the interactive notebook. It makes referencing previously created pages quick and easy for students. Make sure that students leave several pages at the beginning of each notebook for a table of contents.

Expectations and Grading Rubric

It is helpful for each student to have a copy of the expectations for creating interactive notebook pages. You may choose to include a list of expectations for parents and students to sign, as well as a grading rubric (page 11).

Unit Title Pages

Consider using a single page at the beginning of each section to separate it. Title the page with the unit name. Add a tab (page 78) to the edge of the page to make it easy to flip to the unit. Add a table of contents for only the pages in that unit.

Glossary

Reserve a six-page section at the back of the notebook where students can create a glossary. Draw a line to split in half the front and back of each page, creating 24 sections. Combine Q and R and Y and Z to fit the entire alphabet. Have students add an entry as each new vocabulary word is introduced.

Formatting Student Notebook Pages

The other major consideration for planning an interactive notebook is how to treat the left and right sides of a notebook spread. Interactive journals are usually viewed with the notebook open flat. This creates a left side and a right side. You have several options for how to treat the two sides of the spread.

Traditionally, the right side is used for the teacher-directed part of the lesson, and the left side is used for students to interact with the lesson content. The lessons in this book use this format. However, you may prefer to switch the order for your class so that the teacher-directed learning is on the left and the student input is on the right.

It can also be important to include standards, learning objectives, or essential questions in interactive notebooks. You may choose to write these on the top-left side of each page before completing the teacher-directed page on the right side. You may also choose to have students include the "Introduction" part of each lesson in that same top-left section. This is the *in, through, out* method. Students enter *in* the lesson on the top left of the page, go *through* the lesson on the right page, and exit *out* of the lesson on the bottom left with a reflection activity.

The following chart details different types of items and activities that you could include on each side.

| Left Side
Student Output | Right Side
Teacher-Directed Learning |
|---|---|
| • learning objectives
• essential questions
• I Can statements
• brainstorming
• making connections
• summarizing
• making conclusions
• practice problems
• opinions
• questions
• mnemonics
• drawings and diagrams | • vocabulary and definitions
• mini-lessons
• folding activities
• steps in a process
• example problems
• notes
• diagrams
• graphic organizers
• hints and tips
• big ideas |

Planning for the Year

Making a general plan for interactive notebooks will help with planning, grading, and testing throughout the year. You do not need to plan every single page, but knowing what topics you will cover and in what order can be helpful in many ways.

Use the Interactive Notebook Plan (page 9) to plan your units and topics and where they should be placed in the notebooks. Remember to include enough pages at the beginning for the non-content pages, such as the title page, table of contents, and grading rubric. You may also want to leave a page at the beginning of each unit to place a mini table of contents for just that section.

In addition, when planning new pages, it can be helpful to sketch the pieces you will need to create. Use the following notebook template and notes to plan new pages.

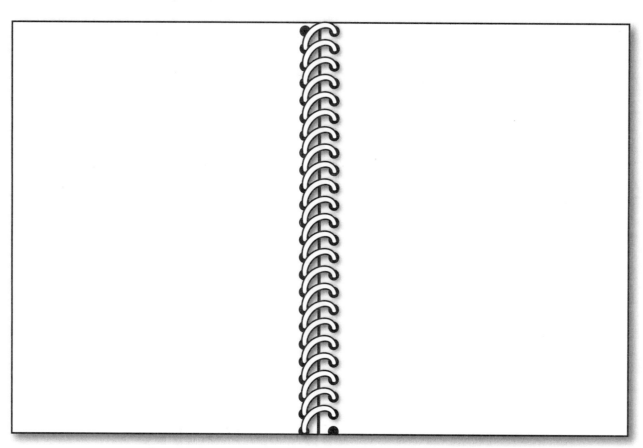

Left Side   **Right Side**

Notes

_____

_____

_____

© Carson-Dellosa • CD-104911

Interactive Notebook Plan

Page	Topic	Page	Topic
1		51	
2		52	
3		53	
4		54	
5		55	
6		56	
7		57	
8		58	
9		59	
10		60	
11		61	
12		62	
13		63	
14		64	
15		65	
16		66	
17		67	
18		68	
19		69	
20		70	
21		71	
22		72	
23		73	
24		74	
25		75	
26		76	
27		77	
28		78	
29		79	
30		80	
31		81	
32		82	
33		83	
34		84	
35		85	
36		86	
37		87	
38		88	
39		89	
40		90	
41		91	
42		92	
43		93	
44		94	
45		95	
46		96	
47		97	
48		98	
49		99	
50		100	

Managing Interactive Notebooks in the Classroom

Working with Younger Students

- Use your yearly plan to preprogram a table of contents that you can copy and give to students to glue into their notebooks, instead of writing individual entries.

- Have assistants or parent volunteers precut pieces.

- Create glue sponges to make gluing easier. Place large sponges in plastic containers with white glue. The sponges will absorb the glue. Students can wipe the backs of pieces across the sponges to apply the glue with less mess.

Creating Notebook Pages

- For storing loose pieces, add a pocket to the inside back cover. Use the envelope pattern (page 81), an envelope, a jumbo library pocket, or a resealable plastic bag. Or, tape the bottom and side edges of the two last pages of the notebook together to create a large pocket.

- When writing under flaps, have students trace the outline of each flap so that they can visualize the writing boundary.

- Where the dashed line will be hidden on the inside of the fold, have students first fold the piece in the opposite direction so that they can see the dashed line. Then, students should fold the piece back the other way along the same fold line to create the fold in the correct direction.

- To avoid losing pieces, have students keep all of their scraps on their desks until they have finished each page.

- To contain paper scraps and avoid multiple trips to the trash can, provide small groups with small buckets or tubs.

- For students who run out of room, keep full and half sheets available. Students can glue these to the bottom of the pages and fold them up when not in use.

Dealing with Absences

- Create a model notebook for absent students to reference when they return to school.

- Have students cut a second set of pieces as they work on their own pages.

Using the Notebook

- To organize sections of the notebook, provide each student with a sheet of tabs (page 78).

- To easily find the next blank page, either cut off the top-right corner of each page as it is used or attach a long piece of yarn or ribbon to the back cover to be used as a bookmark.

Interactive Notebook Grading Rubric

4

_____ Table of contents is complete.

_____ All notebook pages are included.

_____ All notebook pages are complete.

_____ Notebook pages are neat and organized.

_____ Information is correct.

_____ Pages show personalization, evidence of learning, and original ideas.

3

_____ Table of contents is mostly complete.

_____ One notebook page is missing.

_____ Notebook pages are mostly complete.

_____ Notebook pages are mostly neat and organized.

_____ Information is mostly correct.

_____ Pages show some personalization, evidence of learning, and original ideas.

2

_____ Table of contents is missing a few entries.

_____ A few notebook pages are missing.

_____ A few notebook pages are incomplete.

_____ Notebook pages are somewhat messy and unorganized.

_____ Information has several errors.

_____ Pages show little personalization, evidence of learning, or original ideas.

1

_____ Table of contents is incomplete.

_____ Many notebook pages are missing.

_____ Many notebook pages are incomplete.

_____ Notebook pages are too messy and unorganized to use.

_____ Information is incorrect.

_____ Pages show no personalization, evidence of learning, or original ideas.

Integers and Absolute Value

Introduction

Write *+3* and *−3* on the board. Have students discuss the relationship between the numbers. Draw a number line on the board and have students describe where each number should be placed. Distribute index cards with other integer pairs. Have each student find the student with her opposite number. Then, have them add each pair of integers to the number line.

Creating the Notebook Page

Guide students through the following steps to complete the right-hand page in their notebooks.

1. Add a Table of Contents entry for the Integers and Absolute Value pages.

2. Cut out the title and glue it to the top of the page.

3. Cut out the flap book. Cut on the solid line to create two flaps. Apply glue to the back of the top section and attach it to the page below the title.

4. Cut out the two definition pieces and complete the definitions. (a **positive** or **negative whole** number; the **magnitude** of a **number** based on its **distance** from **zero**) Glue each square under the appropriate flap.

5. Cut out one of the number lines. Fold in on the dashed lines. Apply glue to the back of the center section and attach it to the page below the flap book, leaving a few lines of space between.

6. Cut out the four pairs of opposite integers. Glue each integer to the appropriate place on the number line.

7. Shade each set of opposite values with a different color. Then, draw color-coded arrows from zero to each value. Discuss how opposite quantities always have a sum of zero.

8. Cut out the remaining number line. Fold in on the dashed lines. Apply glue to the back of the center section and attach it to the page below the first number line.

9. Cut out the remaining numbers. Glue each absolute value to the correct place on the number line.

Reflect on Learning

To complete the left-hand page, have students describe two situations in which integers can be used in real life. Then, have students describe two situations in which absolute value can be used in real life.

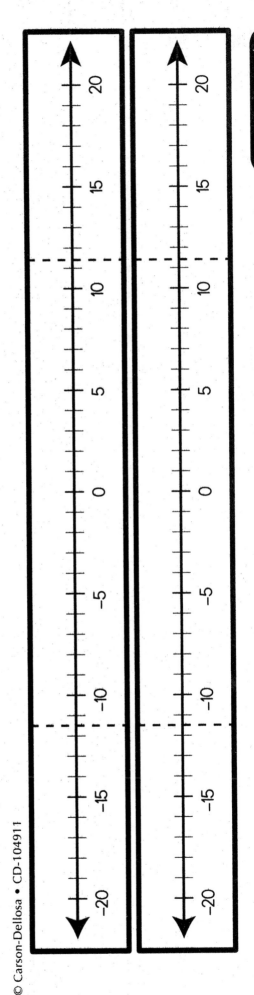

Integers and Absolute Value

Integer	Absolute Value

a_____
or_____
_____
number

the_____
of a_____
based on its
_____
from_____

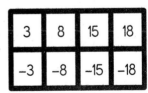

Working with Rational Numbers

Introduction

Write *2, 5, $\frac{7}{8}$, 0.25, 1$\frac{2}{5}$,* and *6.78* on the board. Then, have students work with partners to sort them into three categories. Have them identify what is similar and different about each group and share their thinking with the class. Explain that although these numbers are written in different forms, they all can be described as rational numbers.

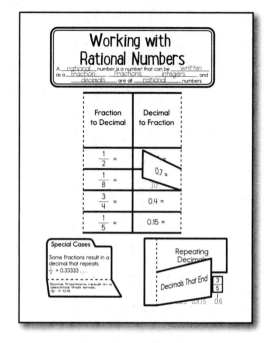

Creating the Notebook Page

Guide students through the following steps to complete the right-hand page in their notebooks.

1. Add a Table of Contents entry for the Working With Rational Numbers pages.

2. Cut out the title and glue it to the top of the page.

3. Complete the explanation. (A **rational** number is a number that can be **written** as a **fraction**. **Fractions**, **integers**, and **decimals** are all **rational** numbers.)

4. Cut out the shutter fold piece. Cut on the solid lines to create ten flaps. Flip over the piece so that the blank side is faceup. Fold each flap in on the dashed lines. Flip the piece back over and apply glue to the gray glue section. Attach the shutter fold to the page below the title.

5. Open the top two flaps and write the steps to convert between number forms. (Fraction to Decimal: 1. Rewrite as a division problem. 2. Divide. Decimal to Fraction: 1. Rewrite the digits over the appropriate power of 10. 2. Simplify.) Then, convert the number on each flap and write the answer under the flap.

6. Cut out the *Special Cases* folder. Fold in on the dashed line. Apply glue to the back of the folder and attach it to the bottom left side of the page.

7. Cut out the flap book. Cut on the solid line to create two flaps. Apply glue to the back of the left section and attach it to the bottom right side of the page.

8. Cut out the fraction pieces and glue each one under the correct flap. Then, convert each fraction to a decimal.

Reflect on Learning

To complete the left-hand page, have students explain why it is helpful to convert between number forms. Have students explain two real-life situations in which they might use this skill.

Answer Key

Repeating Decimals: $\frac{2}{3}$, 0.666666; $\frac{1}{12}$, 0.083333; $\frac{1}{6}$, 0.166666; Decimals That End: $\frac{1}{4}$, 0.25; $\frac{7}{8}$, 0.875; $\frac{3}{5}$, 0.6

Working with Rational Numbers

A _____ number is a number that can be _____ as a _____ . _____ , _____ , and _____ are all _____ numbers.

Decimal to Fraction	glue	Fraction to Decimal
0.25 =		$\frac{1}{2}$ =
0.7 =		$\frac{1}{8}$ =
0.4 =		$\frac{3}{4}$ =
0.15 =		$\frac{1}{5}$ =

Special Cases

Some fractions result in a decimal that repeats. $\frac{1}{3}$ = 0.33333 . . .

Some fractions result in a decimal that ends. $\frac{1}{2}$ = 0.5

Repeating Decimals

Decimals That End

$\frac{2}{3}$	$\frac{1}{4}$
$\frac{7}{8}$	$\frac{1}{12}$
$\frac{1}{6}$	$\frac{3}{5}$

Adding Integers

Introduction

Draw a number line on the board that runs from 0 to 8. Demonstrate how to use the number line to find the sum of 3 + 5. Draw a number line on the board that runs from 0 to −8. Have students work with partners to find the sum of −3 + (−5) and mark their answers on the number line. Allow time for students to explain their answers to the class.

Creating the Notebook Page

Guide students through the following steps to complete the right-hand page in their notebooks.

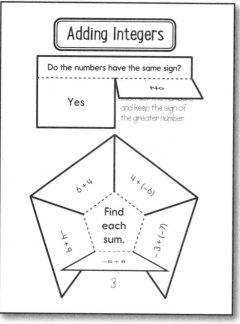

1. Add a Table of Contents entry for the Adding Integers pages.

2. Cut out the title and glue it to the top of the page.

3. Cut out the *Do the numbers have the same sign?* flap book. Cut on the solid line to create two flaps. Apply glue to the back of the top section and attach it to the page below the title.

4. Under each flap, write the procedure for adding integers. (Yes: Add the numbers and keep the sign. No: Subtract the numbers and take the sign of the greater number.)

5. Cut out the pentagon-shaped flap book. Cut on the solid lines to create five flaps. Apply glue to the back of the center section and attach it to the bottom of the page.

6. Solve each problem and write the answer under the flap.

Reflect on Learning

To complete the left-hand page, have students solve the following problems to illustrate integer addition using number lines: 5 + (−3); −8 + 2; −2 + (−7).

Answer Key
Clockwise from top left: 10; −2; −10; 3; 5

Adding Integers

Do the numbers have the same sign?

| Yes | No |

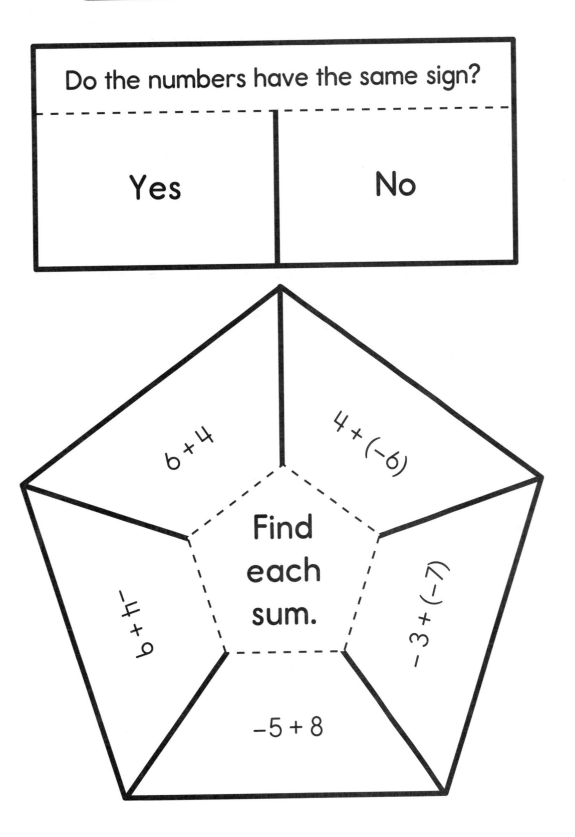

6 + 4

4 + (-6)

Find each sum.

-4 + 9

-3 + (-7)

-5 + 8

Subtracting Integers

Introduction

Write –3 on the board. Have students work in small groups to brainstorm different ways they could describe this number. Answers may include: *the negative sign could represent subtraction, as in 5 – 3; the number could be described as 3 places below zero on a number line;* and *the number could be described as the opposite, or additive inverse, of 3.*

Creating the Notebook Page

Guide students through the following steps to complete the right-hand page in their notebooks.

1. Add a Table of Contents entry for the Subtracting Integers pages.

2. Cut out the title and glue it to the top of the page.

3. Complete the explanation. (To **subtract** integers, use integer **addition** and the **additive inverse** of the **subtrahend**.)

4. Cut out the star. Glue it on the top left side of the page.

5. Cut out the smaller rectangle. Apply glue to the back of it and place it on the top right side of the page.

6. Discuss the meaning of the hint on the star. (Change the operation to addition by adding a line to the subtraction symbol and then change the sign of the integer.) Then, use a colored pen or pencil to change each integer subtraction problem to an addition problem with the additive inverse of the subtrahend.

7. Cut out the flap book. Cut on the solid lines to create six flaps. Apply glue to the back of the left section and attach it to the bottom of the page.

8. On each flap, rewrite the problem from the left column as an addition problem with the additive inverse as the subtrahend. Then, solve the problem under the flap.

Reflect on Learning

To complete the left-hand page, have students explain why the additive inverse has to be used when subtracting integers.

Answer Key
$-6 + 5 = -1$; $-3 + (-13) = -16$; $-6 + (-9) = -15$; $5 + (-18) = -13$; $-1 + 11 = 10$; $32 + (-35) = -3$

Subtracting Integers

To __subtract__ integers, use integer __addition__ and the __additive__ __inverse__ of the __subtrahend__.

Add a line and change the sign.

$4 + (-6)$	$-3 + (-2)$
$-5 + (+7)$	$6 + (+3)$

Solve each problem.

$-6 - (-5)$	$-6+5$
$-3 - 13$	$-3+(-13)$
$-6 - 9$	$-6+(-9)$
$5 - 18$	$5+(-18)$
$-1 - (-11)$	$-1+11$
$32 - 35$	$32+(-35)$

Subtracting Integers

To _____ integers, use integer _____ and the _____ _____ of the _____ .

Add a line and change the sign.

4 – 6	–3 – 2
–5 – (–7)	6 – (–3)

Solve each problem.

–6 – (–5)	
–3 – 13	
–6 – 9	
5 – 18	
–1 – (–11)	
32 – 35	

Adding and Subtracting Using Mathematical Properties

Introduction

Review the associative, commutative, equality, and identity properties. Then, write *4 + 1 + 5* on the board. Have students work with partners to brainstorm different ways to write the expression without changing its value.

Creating the Notebook Page

Guide students through the following steps to complete the right-hand page in their notebooks.

1. Add a Table of Contents entry for the Adding and Subtracting Using Mathematical Properties pages.

2. Cut out the title and glue it to the top of the page.

3. Cut out the four flap books. Cut on the solid lines to create three flaps on each. Apply glue to back of each left section and attach it to the page.

4. Under the first flap of each flap book, write a definition of the property and indicate which operations it is used for. (Associative: when three or more numbers are added, the sum is the same regardless of how the addends are grouped; addition; Commutative: when two or more numbers are added, the sum is the same regardless of the order of the addends; addition; Equality: A number can be added or subtracted on both sides to get an equal equation; addition and subtraction; Identity: the sum or difference of any number and zero is the original number; addition and subtraction)

5. Cut out the example pieces. Glue each example under the correct flap.

Reflect on Learning

To complete the left-hand page, have students write and label two more examples for each property.

Adding and Subtracting Using Mathematical Properties

Associative

Example | Operation | Definition

Commutative

Example | Operation | Definition

Equality

Example | Operation | Definition

Identity

Example | Operation | Definition

$\left(\dfrac{3}{4} + \dfrac{1}{2}\right) + \dfrac{4}{5} = \dfrac{3}{4} + \left(\dfrac{1}{2} + \dfrac{4}{5}\right)$	If $37 + 29 = 66$, then $37 + 29 + 84 = 66 + 84$
$6.59 + 7.42 = 7.42 + 6.59$	$\dfrac{7}{8} - 0 = \dfrac{7}{8}$

Adding and Subtracting Rational Numbers

Introduction

Write $\frac{1}{2}$ on the board. Ask students to write the fraction in different forms and allow them to share their answers with the class. Then, write $\frac{1}{2} + 0.5$ on the board. Have students discuss with partners possible ways to solve the problem.

Creating the Notebook Page

Guide students through the following steps to complete the right-hand page in their notebooks.

1. Add a Table of Contents entry for the Adding and Subtracting Rational Numbers pages.

2. Cut out the title and glue it to the top of the page.

3. Cut out the *Step 1* piece. Fold the top and bottom sections in on the dashed lines. Apply glue to the back of the center section and attach it to the top left of the page. Label the piece *Steps to Follow*.

4. Cut out the *Hints* folder. Fold in on the dashed line. Apply glue to the back of the folder and attach it to the top right of the page.

5. Cut out the three flap books. Cut on the solid lines to create five flaps on each. Apply glue to the gray glue sections and stack the pieces directly on top of each other with the *Show your steps and solve* piece on top. Apply glue to the back of the left section and attach the stacked flap book to the bottom of the page.

6. Solve each problem and show the steps for each problem on the flaps.

Reflect on Learning

To complete the left-hand page, have students explain why rational numbers have to be converted to the same form before adding or subtracting. Have students illustrate their explanations using examples of real-life problems.

Answer Key

From top: $-\frac{6}{8} - \frac{4}{5} = -\frac{30}{40} - \frac{32}{40} = -\frac{62}{40} = -\frac{31}{20} = -1\frac{11}{20}$; $3.1 + \frac{8}{4} = 3\frac{1}{10} + \frac{8}{4} = 3\frac{2}{20} + \frac{40}{20} = 3\frac{2}{20} = 5\frac{1}{10}$;

$24 - (-\frac{9}{8}) = 24 + \frac{9}{8} = \frac{192}{8} + \frac{9}{8} = \frac{201}{8} = 25\frac{1}{8}$; $5.8 - (-2) = 5.8 + 2 = 5.8 = 2.0 = 7.8$; $4.3 + \frac{2}{6} = 4\frac{3}{10} + \frac{2}{6} = 4\frac{9}{30} + \frac{10}{30} = 4\frac{19}{30}$

Adding and Subtracting Rational Numbers

Hints

- Add and subtract positive and negative fractions the same way as you would whole number integers.

- Convert rational numbers to the same form to add or subtract.

Step 1: Evaluate
Are the numbers in the same form?
Are negative subtrahends used?
Do fractions have a common denominator?

Step 2: Convert
Change numbers to the same form. Use the additive inverse and addition for negative subtrahends.

Step 3: Solve
Find the answer to the problem. Simplify.

glue

glue

Show your steps and solve.

$-\dfrac{6}{8} - \dfrac{4}{5}$	$3.1 + \dfrac{8}{4}$	$24 - \left(-\dfrac{9}{8}\right)$	$5.8 - (-2)$	$4.3 + \dfrac{2}{6}$

Multiplying Fractions and Mixed Numbers

Introduction

Write $\frac{3}{4} \times 8$ on the board. Have students work with partners to determine different ways to solve the problem. Allow time for students to share their thinking.

Creating the Notebook Page

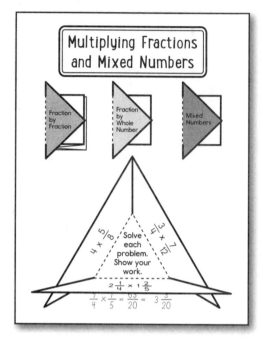

Guide students through the following steps to complete the right-hand page in their notebooks.

1. Add a Table of Contents entry for the Multiplying Fractions and Mixed Numbers pages.

2. Cut out the title and glue it to the top of the page.

3. Cut out the three accordion folds. For each piece, fold back and forth on the dashed lines to create an accordion with the arrow on top. Apply glue to the back of each last section. Attach them below the title in a row.

4. Follow the steps to solve the problem shown on the last section of each arrow. If desired, color code the sections and each step of the process to match.

5. Cut out the triangle flap book. Cut on the solid lines to create three flaps. Apply glue to the back of the center triangle and attach it to the bottom of the page.

6. Use the steps from the accordion fold pieces to solve each problem and write the answers under the flap.

Reflect on Learning

To complete the left-hand page, have students create three real-life problems using multiplication of fractions and mixed numbers. Then, have students trade notebooks and solve partners' problems.

Answer Key
Clockwise from left: $2\frac{1}{2}$; $\frac{7}{16}$; $3\frac{3}{20}$

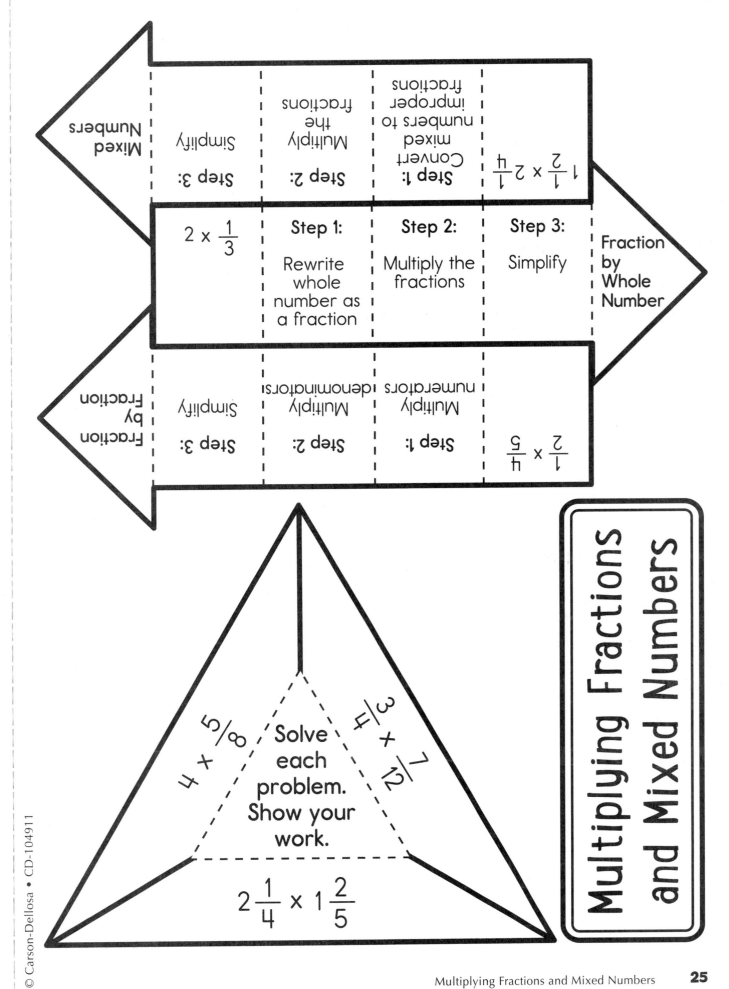

Mixed Numbers

Step 3: Simplify

Step 2: Multiply the fractions

Step 1: Convert mixed numbers to improper fractions

$1\frac{1}{2} \times 2\frac{1}{4}$

$2 \times \frac{1}{3}$

Step 1: Rewrite whole number as a fraction

Step 2: Multiply the fractions

Step 3: Simplify

Fraction by Whole Number

Fraction by Fraction

Step 3: Simplify

Step 2: Multiply denominators

Step 1: Multiply numerators

$\frac{1}{2} \times \frac{4}{5}$

$4 \times \frac{5}{8}$

$\frac{3}{4} \times \frac{7}{12}$

Solve each problem. Show your work.

$2\frac{1}{4} \times 1\frac{2}{5}$

Multiplying Fractions and Mixed Numbers

Multiplying and Dividing Using Mathematical Properties

Introduction

Review the properties of addition. Write *(7 + 2) + 4, 7 + 8*, and *3 + 0* on the board. Have students use what they have learned about the mathematical properties of addition to write an equivalent expression for each expression. Allow students to share their answers and explain their reasoning.

Creating the Notebook Page

Guide students through the following steps to complete the right-hand page in their notebooks.

1. Add a Table of Contents entry for the Multiplying and Dividing Using Mathematical Properties pages.

2. Cut out the title and glue it to the top of the page.

3. Cut out the properties flap book. Cut on the solid lines to create six flaps. Apply glue to the back of the left section and attach it to the top of the page.

4. Under each flap, write how each property is used in the operation or operations that are shown on the top of the flap.

5. Cut out the *Which Property?* flap book. Cut on the solid lines to create four flaps on each side. Apply glue to the center section and attach it to the bottom of the page.

6. Cut out the eight property pieces. Glue each one under the correct flap to identify the property shown in each expression.

Multiplying and Dividing Using Mathematical Properties

Associative	x	
Commutative	x	
Identity	x	÷
Inverse	x	
Zero	x	÷
Distributive	x	

	Which Property?	
436 x 1 = 436		4 x 234 = (4 x 200) + (4 x 30) + (4 x 4)
0 ÷ 98 = 0		(43 x 29) x 61 = 43 x (29 x 61)
$25 \times \frac{1}{25} = 1$		36.8 x 0 = 0
$37 \times \frac{6}{5} = \frac{6}{5} \times 37$		569 ÷ 1 = 569

Reflect on Learning

To complete the left-hand page, have students explain why understanding the mathematical properties of multiplication and division is important.

Answer Key

$436 \times 1 = 436$: identity; $0 \div 98 = 0$: zero; $25 \times \frac{1}{25} = 1$. inverse; $37 \times \frac{6}{5} = \frac{6}{5} \times 37$: commutative; $4 \times 234 = (4 \times 200) + (4 \times 30) + (4 \times 4)$: distributive; $(43 \times 29) \times 61 = 43 \times (29 \times 61)$: associative; $36.8 \times 0 = 0$: zero; $569 \div 1 = 569$: identity

Multiplying and Dividing Using Mathematical Properties

Associative	X	
Commutative	X	
Identity	X	÷
Inverse	X	
Zero	X	÷
Distributive	X	

associative
commutative
identity
identity
inverse
zero
zero

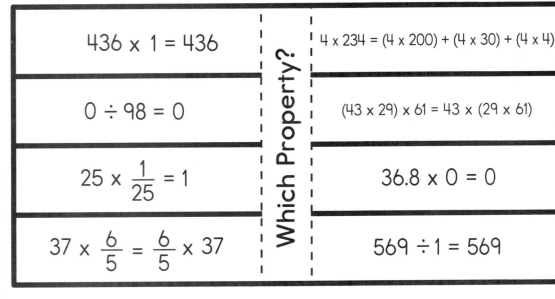

	Which Property?	
436 x 1 = 436		4 x 234 = (4 x 200) + (4 x 30) + (4 x 4)
0 ÷ 98 = 0		(43 x 29) x 61 = 43 x (29 x 61)
25 x $\frac{1}{25}$ = 1		36.8 x 0 = 0
37 x $\frac{6}{5}$ = $\frac{6}{5}$ x 37		569 ÷ 1 = 569

distributive

Multiplying Integers

Introduction

Pass out index cards with simple multiplication problems (such as 3 × 2). Have students work with partners to rewrite each problem using addition (for example, 2 + 2 + 2). Remind students that multiplication of positive integers is repeated addition.

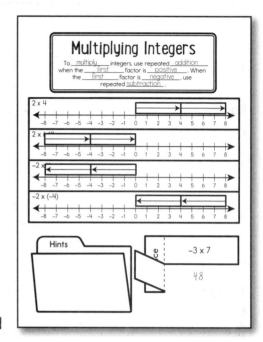

Creating the Notebook Page

Guide students through the following steps to complete the right-hand page in their notebooks.

1. Add a Table of Contents entry for the Multiplying Integers pages.

2. Cut out the title and glue it to the top of the page.

3. Complete the sentences under the title. (To **multiply** integers, use repeated **addition** when the **first** factor is **positive**. When the **first** factor is **negative**, use repeated **subtraction**.)

4. Cut out the four number lines and glue them at the top of the page, one below the other.

5. Cut out the small arrows and glue them above each number line to show the product of each example problem.

6. Cut out the *Hints* folder. Fold in on the dashed line. Apply glue to the back of the folder and attach it to the bottom left of the page.

7. Cut out the *Practice* flap book. Cut on the solid line to create two flaps. Apply glue to the back of the left section and attach it to the bottom right of the page.

8. Solve each problem and write the answer under the flap.

Reflect on Learning

To complete the left-hand page, have students draw number lines to model how each problem from the practice flap book can be solved using repeated addition or subtraction.

Answer Key
From top: −21; 48

2 x 4

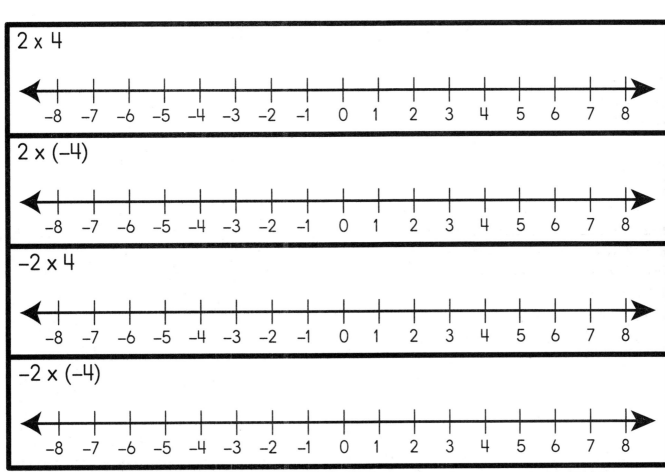

2 x (−4)

−2 x 4

−2 x (−4)

Multiplying Integers

To _____ integers, use repeated _____ when the _____ factor is _____. When the _____ factor is _____, use repeated _____.

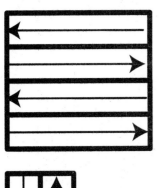

Practice

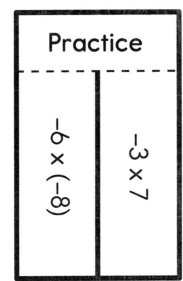

−6 x (−8)

−3 x 7

Hints

Same Signs: Positive Product

Different Signs: Negative Product

Dividing Integers

Introduction

Write *−4 × 2* on the board and allow time for students to solve the problem. As a class, discuss inverse operations. Remind students that division is the inverse operation of multiplication. Write *−8 ÷ 2* on the board. Ask students to use what they know about multiplication of integers and inverse operations to predict the quotient. Then, allow students to share and explain their predictions.

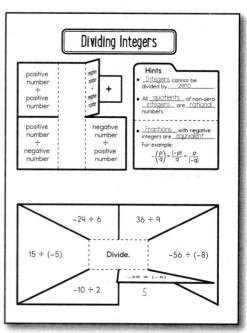

Creating the Notebook Page

Guide students through the following steps to complete the right-hand page in their notebooks.

1. Add a Table of Contents entry for the Dividing Integers pages.

2. Cut out the title and glue it to the top of the page.

3. Cut out the *positive number* flap book. Cut on the solid lines to create four flaps. Apply glue to the back of the center section and attach it to the top left side of the page.

4. Cut out the four positive and negative symbol pieces. Glue each one under the correct flap.

5. Cut out the *Hints* folder. Fold in on the dashed line. Apply glue to the back of the folder and attach it to the top right of the page.

6. Complete the sentences in the *Hints* folder. (**Integers** cannot be divided by **zero**. All **quotients** of non-zero **integers** are **rational** numbers. **Fractions** with negative integers are **equivalent**.)

7. Cut out the *Divide* flap book. Cut on the solid lines to create six flaps. Apply glue to the center section and attach it to the bottom of the page.

8. Solve each problem and write the answer under the flap.

Reflect on Learning

To complete the left-hand page, have students write two real-world word problems involving integer division. Then, have students trade notebooks with partners and solve the problems.

Answer Key:
Clockwise from top left: −4; 4; 7; 5; −5; −3

Dividing Integers

positive number ÷ positive number

negative number ÷ negative number

positive number ÷ negative number

negative number ÷ positive number

Hints

- _____ cannot be divided by _____ .

- All _____ of non-zero _____ are _____ numbers.

- _____ with negative integers are _____ .
  For example:
  $$-\left(\frac{p}{q}\right) = \frac{(-p)}{q} = \frac{p}{(-q)}$$

| - | - | + | + |

−24 ÷ 6

36 ÷ 9

15 ÷ (−5)

Divide.

−56 ÷ (−8)

−10 ÷ 2

−25 ÷ (−5)

Unit Rates with Fractions

Introduction

Review equivalent fractions with students by writing $\frac{2}{3} = \frac{4}{6}$ and $\frac{3}{4} = \frac{7}{8}$ on the board. Have students work with a partner to determine if each statement is true. Explain that when finding unit rates with fractions, it is important that equivalent fractions or ratios are used.

Creating the Notebook Page

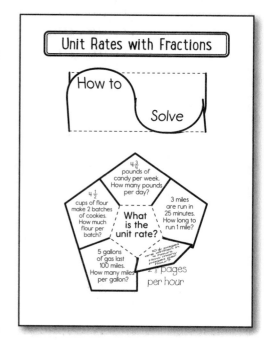

Guide students through the following steps to complete the right-hand page in their notebooks.

1. Add a Table of Contents entry for the Unit Rates with Fractions pages.

2. Cut out the title and glue it to the top of the page.

3. Cut out the interlocking booklet. With the blank side faceup, fold the top and bottom in on the dashed lines. Apply glue to the gray glue section and attach it below the title.

4. Take notes about solving unit rates with fractions inside the booklet. (1. Set up equivalent ratios using given information and a 1 for the unit rate you are trying to find. 2. Cross-multiply. 3. Solve for the unknown quantity. Hint: Make sure units for numerators and denominators stay the same.)

5. Cut out the flap book. Cut on the solid lines to create five flaps. Apply glue to the back of the center section and attach it to the bottom of the page.

6. Find each unit rate described and write the answer under the flap.

Reflect on Learning

To complete the left-hand page, have students identify a real-life scenario in which unit rates are used. Student should identify the unit rate and create a table using several values based on that unit rate.

Answer Key
Clockwise from top: $\frac{19}{28}$ of a pound; $8\frac{1}{3}$ minutes or 8 minutes and 20 seconds; $2\frac{5}{8}$ pages; 20 miles; $2\frac{1}{4}$ cups of flour

Unit Rates with Fractions

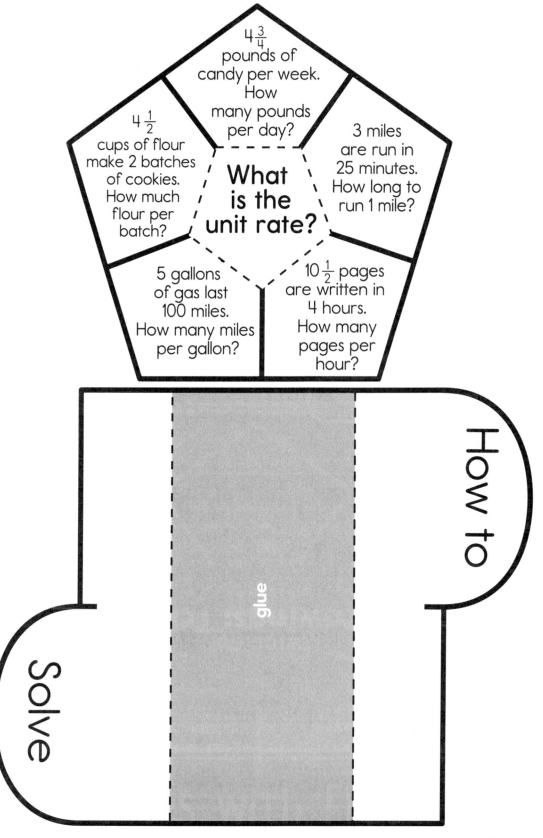

$4\frac{3}{4}$ pounds of candy per week. How many pounds per day?

$4\frac{1}{2}$ cups of flour make 2 batches of cookies. How much flour per batch?

3 miles are run in 25 minutes. How long to run 1 mile?

What is the unit rate?

5 gallons of gas last 100 miles. How many miles per gallon?

$10\frac{1}{2}$ pages are written in 4 hours. How many pages per hour?

How to

Solve

glue

Testing Proportional Relationships

Introduction

Have students think about making cookies. Ask: *If one recipe makes 12 cookies, and I need 24 cookies, what do I need to do to the recipe?* When students reply that you would need to make two batches of cookies or double the recipe, point out that when you double the amount of flour in the recipe, you would also need to double the amount of sugar. If not, the cookies would not come out sweet enough. Explain to students that when a recipe is doubled, proportional relationships have to be used.

Creating the Notebook Page

Guide students through the following steps to complete the right-hand page in their notebooks.

1. Add a Table of Contents entry for the Testing Proportional Relationships pages.

2. Cut out the title and glue it to the top of the page.

3. Complete the sentence below the title. (A **proportional** relationship is present between **two** or more **equal** ratios.)

4. Cut out the *Graphing* and *Equal Ratios* flaps. Apply glue to the back of the left sections and attach them below the title.

5. Cut out the example rectangles and glue them under the correct flaps. Follow the steps to complete each example.

6. Cut out the *Is this proportional?* flap books. For each flap book, cut on the solid lines to create two flaps. Then, apply glue to the back of the top left section and attach it to the bottom of the page.

7. Answer each question by writing *yes* or *no* under the flap. Then, explain your answer under the flap using graphing or equal ratios.

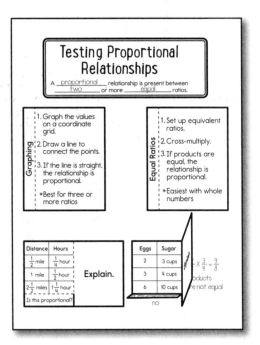

Reflect on Learning

To complete the left-hand page, have students create a new set of values for a real world situation. Next, have students set up a table with the values. Then, students should ask a partner to test the proportional relationship between the values.

Answer Key
Distance and Hours: Yes
Eggs and Sugar: No

Testing Proportional Relationships

A _____ relationship is present between _____ or more _____ ratios.

Equal Ratios

1. Set up equivalent ratios.
2. Cross-multiply.
3. If products are equal, the relationship is proportional.

*Easiest with whole numbers

Graphing

1. Graph the values on a coordinate grid.
2. Draw a line to connect the points.
3. If the line is straight, the relationship is proportional.

*Best for three or more ratios

Example:

x	2	4
y	1	2

Example:

x	2	6	10
y	4	12	20

Distance	Hours
$\frac{1}{2}$ mile	$\frac{1}{4}$ hour
1 mile	$\frac{1}{2}$ hour
$2\frac{1}{2}$ miles	$1\frac{1}{4}$ hour

Is this proportional?

Explain.

Eggs	Sugar
2	3 cups
3	4 cups
6	10 cups

Is this proportional?

Explain.

© Carson-Dellosa • CD-104911

Constants of Proportionality

Introduction

Remind students about proportional relationships by creating a table with *x* values of 2, 4, and 6 and *y* values of 4, 8, and 12. Ask students to work with partners to determine whether the relationship among these values is proportional. Once they determine that it is proportional, ask them to predict what the *y* value will be if the *x* value is 8.

Creating the Notebook Page

Guide students through the following steps to complete the right-hand page in their notebooks.

1. Add a Table of Contents entry for the Constants of Proportionality pages.

2. Cut out the title and glue it to the top of the page.

3. Cut out the *What Is It?* flap book. Cut on the solid lines to create three flaps. Apply glue to the back of the left section and attach it below the title.

4. Answer each question under the appropriate flap. (a ratio that stays the same for many relationships; $k = y/x$; $y = kx$ when k = constant of proportionality)

5. Cut out the four practice flap books. For each flap book, cut on the solid line to create two flaps. Apply glue to the back of the left sections and attach them to the bottom of the page.

6. Find the constant of proportionality and test it under the flaps on each practice square.

Reflect on Learning

To complete the left-hand page, have students create a proportional value table in which the first *y* values are 0 and 5 and the first *x* values are 1 and 2. Have students determine the constant of proportionality and add 3 more proportional values to each column to complete the table.

Answer Key
For $y = 2$ and $x = 1$, $k = 2$; For $y = 2$ and $x = 10$, $k = \frac{1}{5}$; For $y = 1$ and $x = 5$, $k = \frac{1}{5}$; For $y = 3$ and $x = 1$, $k = 3$

Constants of Proportionality

What is it?

How do I write it?

How can I test it?

y	x	Constant of Proportionality
2	1	
4	2	
6	3	Test It
8	4	

y	x	Constant of Proportionality
2	10	
4	20	
6	30	Test It
8	40	

y	x	Constant of Proportionality
1	5	
2	10	
3	15	Test It
4	20	

y	x	Constant of Proportionality
3	1	
6	2	
9	3	Test It
12	4	

Using Variables

Introduction

Write these problems on the board: *3 + ? = 5, 6 − ? = 4,*
5 × ? = 30, 18 ÷ ? = 9. Have students work with partners to discuss
what value belongs in the place of each question mark. Allow time
for students to share their findings. Explain to students that they
have just used what they know about math problems to solve for
variables.

Creating the Notebook Page

Guide students through the following steps to complete the
right-hand page in their notebooks.

1. Add a Table of Contents entry for the Using Variables
   pages.

2. Cut out the title and glue it to the top of the page.

3. Cut out the *Variable* flap book. Cut on the solid lines to
   create four flaps. Apply glue to the back of the center
   section and attach it below the title.

4. Cut out the four large rectangle pieces. Glue each one under the correct flap. Under the
   Example flap, circle or highlight the variables. Complete the sentences under the *Definition*
   and *Facts* flaps. (Definition: a **letter** or **symbol** that represents a **value** in an **expression** or
   equation; Facts: represents a **number**, can be a **letter** or a **symbol**, **expressions** can have
   more than one)

5. Cut out the *Words/Expressions* piece and glue it below the *Variable* flap book. Continue the
   center line down the page to create a two-column chart.

6. Cut out the eight small rectangles. Match each expression with a phrase. Then, glue each
   piece to the correct side of the chart.

7. Circle or highlight the variable in each expression. Discuss how the variable was used to
   replace the unknown number in each expression.

Reflect on Learning

To complete the left-hand page, have students write a word problem with an unknown value. Then,
have students write an equation to solve the problem.

38

Using Variables (notebook diagram)

Definition	Facts
Examples	◇ Variable ◇
3x + y	Non-Examples

Words	Expressions
seven less than a number	$(x) - 7$
eight more than a number	$8 + (b)$
ten divided by a number	$10 ÷ (a)$
three times a number	$3 × (c)$

Using Variables

Definition	Facts

Variable

Examples	Non-Examples

Expressions

a _____ or _____ that represents a _____ in an _____ or _____	• represents a _____ • can be a _____ or a _____ • _____ can have more than one
$5n + 3$ $3x + y$	$4 + 6 = 10$ -5

Words

seven less than a number	eight more than a number	three times a number	ten divided by a number	$8 + b$	$3 \times c$	$10 \div a$	$x - 7$

Mathematical Properties and Equivalent Expressions

Introduction

Write *6 + 8 = 14* on the board. Have students work with small groups to write the expression a different way (8 + 6 = 14). Remind students that this is the commutative property of addition. Therefore, 6 + 8 = 8 + 6. These are equivalent expressions.

Creating the Notebook Page

Guide students through the following steps to complete the right-hand page in their notebooks.

1. Add a Table of Contents entry for the Mathematical Properties and Equivalent Expressions pages.

2. Cut out the title and glue it to the top of the page.

3. Cut out the *Examples* flap book. Cut on the solid lines to create three flaps on each side. Apply glue to the back of the center section and attach it below the title.

4. Cut out the six types of properties pieces. Glue each one under the correct flap.

5. Cut out the *Equivalent Expressions* flap book. Cut on the solid lines to create five flaps. Apply glue to the back of the left section and attach it to the bottom of the page.

6. On each flap, write the equivalent expression. Then, write which property was used under the flap.

Mathematical Properties and Equivalent Expressions

$(6 + 7) + 2 = 6 + (7 + 2)$		$4 \times (3 - 1) = (4 \times 3) - (4 \times 1)$
$0 \div 8 = 0$		$423 \times 1 = 423$
commutative		$4 \times 0 = 0$

Examples

Equivalent Expressions

3×2	$\neq$	2×3
$7 \times (4 + 2)$	$\neq$	$(7 \times 4) + (7 \times 2)$
41×1	$\neq$	41
$(4 \times 2) \times 5$	$\neq$	associative
51×0	$\neq$	0

Reflect on Learning

To complete the left-hand page, have students explain why receiving a 15% discount is the same as finding 85 percent of the original cost of an item. Then, have them explain how the mathematical properties and equivalent expressions helped them understand and solve the problem.

Answer Key
From top: Answers will vary but may include 2 × 3, commutative; (7 × 4) + (7 × 2), distributive; 41, identity; 4 × (2 × 5), associative; 0, zero

Mathematical Properties and Equivalent Expressions

	Examples	
$(6 + 7) + 2 = 6 + (7 + 2)$		$4 \times (3 - 1) = (4 \times 3) - (4 \times 1)$
$0 \div 8 = 0$		$423 \times 1 = 423$
$6 + 7 = 7 + 6$		$4 \times 0 = 0$

zero

associative

distributive

zero

identity

commutative

Equivalent Expressions

3×2	$\neq$
$7 \times (4 + 2)$	$\neq$
41×1	$\neq$
$(4 \times 2) \times 5$	$\neq$
51×0	$\neq$

Creating Expressions

Introduction

Have students consider what expression represents the phrase *three more than a number*. Then, allow time for students to discuss and share their ideas with a partner. Call on a volunteer to approach the board and share their thinking. As a class, discuss the expression given and any responses that were different.

Creating the Notebook Page

Guide students through the following steps to complete the right-hand page in their notebooks.

1. Add a Table of Contents entry for the Creating Expressions pages.

2. Cut out the title and glue it to the top of the page.

3. Cut out the *Operation Hints* flap book. Cut on the solid lines to create four flaps. Apply glue to the back of the top section and attach it below the title.

4. Under each flap, record clue words for each mathematical operation.

5. Cut out the *Create expressions* flap book. Cut on the solid lines to create four flaps. Apply glue to the back of the left section and attach it to the bottom left of the page.

6. Under each flap, write an expression that represents the phrase.

7. Cut out the *Describe expressions* flap book. Cut on the solid lines to create four flaps. Apply glue to the back of the left section and attach it to the bottom right of the page.

8. Under each flap, write a phrase to describe the expression.

Creating Expressions

Operation Hints			
addition	subtraction	multiplication	division

Create expressions.

| twelve less than two times a number |
| five times the quotient of six divided by a number |
| ten divided by three times a number |
| a number increased by twenty |

Describe expressions.

| $5x - 23$ |
| $3y \div 2$ |
| a number increased by 51 |
| $4 + (11 \times n)$ |

Reflect on Learning

To complete the left-hand page, write the following problem on the board: *Olivia earns an allowance of $20.00 per week plus $2.00 for every extra chore she completes.* Ask students to write an expression to show how much money Olivia will earn this week if she completes *x* extra chores.

Answer Key
Create Expressions: Answers will vary but may include: $2a - 12$; $5 \times (6 \div x)$; $10 \div (3 \times b)$; $y + 20$
Describe Expressions: Answers will vary but may include the difference between 5 times a number and 23; 3 times a number divided by 2; the sum of 51 and a number; the product of 11 and a number increased by 4.

Creating Expressions

Operation Hints

addition	subtraction	multiplication	division

Create expressions.

twelve less than two times a number

five times the quotient of six divided by a number

ten divided by three times a number

a number increased by twenty

Describe expressions.

$5x - 23$

$3y \div 2$

$n + 51$

$4 + (11 \times n)$

Expressing and Graphing Inequalities

Introduction

Draw a number line that runs from –10 to 10 on the board. Pass out index cards with inequalities such as $x > 3$, $y < –1$, and $5 \geq a$ written on them. Have students draw number lines on the reverse sides of the index cards to graph the given inequalities. Then, allow time for several sets of partners to show their inequalities on the number line on the board.

Creating the Notebook Page

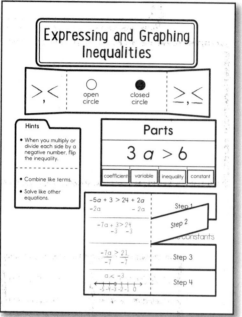

Guide students through the following steps to complete the right-hand page in their notebooks.

1. Add a Table of Contents entry for the Expressing and Graphing Inequalities pages.

2. Cut out the title and glue it to the top of the page.

3. Cut out the *open circle/closed circle* piece. Fold in on the dashed lines so that the flaps meet in the center. Apply glue to the back of the center section and attach it below the title.

4. On each flap, write which symbols are used with open and closed circles. (open circle: >, <; closed circle: ≤, ≥)

5. Cut out the *Hints* folder. Fold in on the dashed line. Apply glue to the back of the folder and attach it to the left side of the page.

6. Cut out the *Parts* rectangle and glue it beside the *Hints* folder. Then, cut out the four small labels and glue each label under the correct part of the inequality.

7. Cut out the flap book. Cut on the solid lines to create four flaps. Apply glue to the back of the left section and attach it to the bottom of the page.

8. Write each step for expressing and graphing inequalities under the flaps. (Step 1: Combine terms with like variables. Step 2: Combine constants. Step 3: Divide or multiply to remove the coefficient. Flip the sign if it is negative. Step 4: Graph using an open or closed circle depending on the type of inequality.) If desired, color each flap a different color.

9. Solve and graph the example inequality.

Reflect on Learning

To complete the left-hand page, have students create and graph four different inequalities. Students should include both open circle and closed circle inequalities.

Expressing and Graphing Inequalities

○ open circle   ● closed circle

inequality	coefficient
variable	constant

Parts

$$3\ a > 6$$

Hints

- When you multiply or divide each side by a negative number, flip the inequality.

- Combine like terms.

- Solve like other equations.

$-5a + 3 > 24 + 2a$

Step 1

Step 2

Step 3

Step 4

Drawing Triangles

Introduction

Provide students with a variety of triangles. Have students work with partners to sort the triangles in various ways. As a class, discuss the different ways each student sorted the triangles.

Creating the Notebook Page

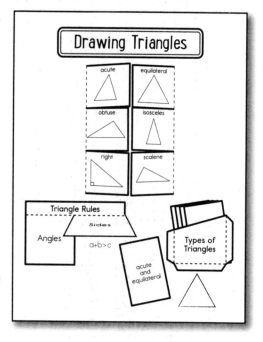

Guide students through the following steps to complete the right-hand page in their notebooks.

1. Add a Table of Contents entry for the Drawing Triangles pages.

2. Cut out the title and glue it to the top of the page.

3. Cut out the shutter fold piece. Cut on the solid lines to create six flaps. Flip over the piece so that the blank side is faceup. Fold each flap in on the dashed lines. Flip the piece back over and apply glue to the gray glue section. Attach the shutter fold to the page below the title.

4. Record notes about each type of triangle under each flap. For example, equilateral triangles have 3 equal sides and 3 equal angles.

5. Cut out the *Triangle Rules* flap book. Cut on the solid line to create two flaps. Apply glue to the back of the top section and attach it to the left side of the page below the shutter fold.

6. Record notes about angles and sides under the appropriate flaps. (Angles: $\angle 1 + \angle 2 + \angle 3 = 180°$; Sides: $a + b > c$)

7. Cut out the *Types of Triangles* pocket. Apply glue to the back of the tabs, and attach it to the page beside the *Triangle Rules* flap book.

8. Cut out the six description cards and store them in the pocket.

9. Choose a card from the pocket. Draw and label a triangle on the page that fits the description given. Repeat this activity with the remaining cards as time allows.

Reflect on Learning

To complete the left-hand page, ask students to look around the classroom. Students should identify five triangles around the classroom and classify them as either equilateral, isosceles, or scalene and acute, equilateral, or right. Then, students should record and describe each triangle.

Drawing Triangles

Triangle Rules

Angles	Sides

Types of Triangles

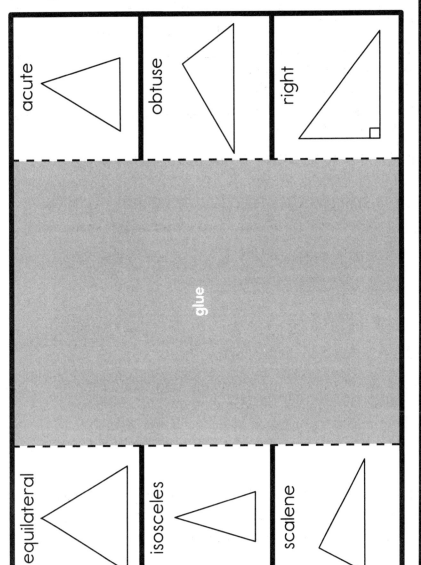

acute

obtuse

right

glue

equilateral

isosceles

scalene

right and scalene	acute and equilateral
scalene and obtuse	isosceles and acute
right and isosceles	isosceles and obtuse

Scale Drawings: Triangles

Introduction

Review similar figures by drawing two equilateral triangles on the board. Make one with 2-unit sides and one with 4-unit sides. Have students work with partners to list qualities that make the triangles similar. As a class, discuss each quality.

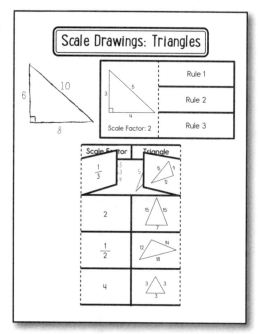

Creating the Notebook Page

Guide students through the following steps to complete the right-hand page in their notebooks.

1. Add a Table of Contents entry for the Scale Drawings: Triangles pages

2. Cut out the title and glue it to the top of the page.

3. Cut out the *Rule 1* flap book. Cut on the solid lines to create three flaps. Apply glue to the back of the left section and attach it to the top right of the page.

4. Record notes about the rules of creating scale drawings under each flap. (Rule 1: same shape, different side lengths; Rule 2: Corresponding sides are proportional using the given scale factor as the constant of proportionality. Rule 3: Corresponding angles are congruent.) Use the triangle and the given scale factor to create a scaled drawing to the left of the flap book.

5. Cut out the shutter fold piece. Cut on the solid lines to create ten flaps. Flip over the piece so that the blank side is faceup. Fold each flap in on the dashed lines. Flip the piece back over and apply glue to the gray glue section. Attach the shutter fold to the page below the title. Apply glue to the back of the *Triangle* and *Scale Factor* flaps and attach them to the piece.

6. Under each set of flaps, use the scale factor to create a scale drawing for each triangle. Label the new lengths.

Reflect on Learning

To complete the left-hand page, have students create four scale drawings of quadrilaterals using a scale factor of their own choosing. Remind students to refer to the rules before creating their drawings.

Answer Key
From top: 5, 3, 4; 30, 30, 14; 6, 7, 9; 12, 12, 12

Scale Drawings: Triangles

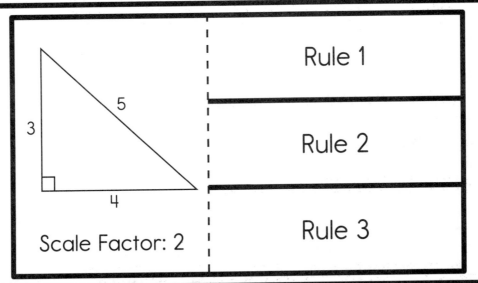

Scale Factor: 2

Rule 1

Rule 2

Rule 3

Triangle		Scale Factor
15 9 12	glue	$\dfrac{1}{3}$
15 15 7		2
12 14 18		$\dfrac{1}{2}$
3 3 3		4

Cross Sections of 3-D Figures

Draw a variety of common 3-D figures on the board or, if available, pass out a variety of 3-D shapes to students. Group students by shape and ask them to describe their assigned shapes using geometric vocabulary. Students might describe the shape of the faces or the number of edges. In addition, ask students to think about the shape of the inside of each 3-D figure. Allow time for each group to share their thoughts with the class.

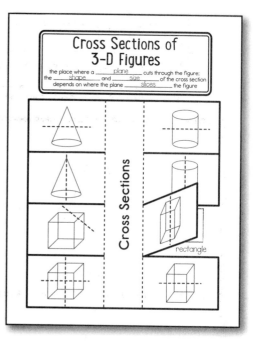

Creating the Notebook Page

Guide students through the following steps to complete the right-hand page in their notebooks.

1. Add a Table of Contents entry for the Cross Sections of 3-D Figures pages.

2. Cut out the title and glue it to the top of the page.

3. Complete the definition. (the place where a **plane** cuts through the figure; the **shape** and **size** of the cross section depends on where the plane **slices** the figure)

4. Cut out the *Cross Sections* flap book. Cut on the solid lines to create eight flaps. Apply glue to the back of the center section and attach it to the page.

5. Under each flap, draw the shape of the cross section created by the image on the flap. Then, label the shape.

Reflect on Learning

To complete the left-hand page, have students draw another type of 3-D figure. Students should draw dotted lines to indicate cross sections. Then, students should name what shapes are created by the cross sections.

Answer Key
From left to right, top to bottom: circle; circle; triangle; rectangle; triangle; rectangle; square; square (or rectangle)

Cross Sections of 3-D Figures

the place where a _____ cuts through the figure;
the _____ and _____ of the cross section
depends on where the plane _____ the figure

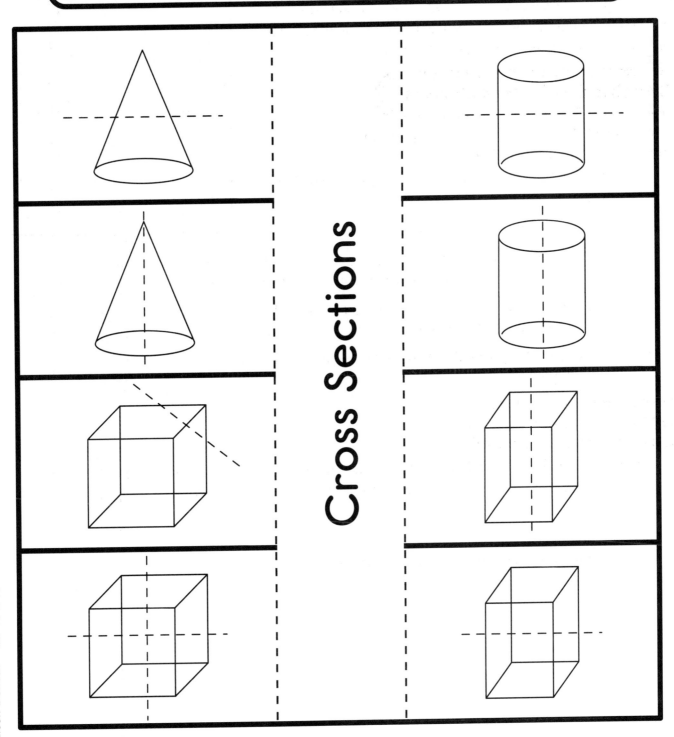

Circumference

Introduction

Draw a circle on the board. Call on volunteers to approach the board and label the parts of a circle (center, radius, diameter, and circumference). As a class, list the characteristics of the circle (a circle is a continuous curve; it is a series of points that are an equal distance from the center, etc.).

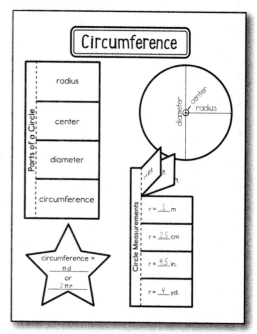

Creating the Notebook Page

Guide students through the following steps to complete the right-hand page in their notebooks.

1. Add a Table of Contents entry for the Circumference pages.

2. Cut out the title and glue it to the top of the page.

3. Cut out the *Parts of a Circle* flap book. Cut on the solid lines to create four flaps. Apply glue to the back of the left section and attach it to the top left side of the page.

4. Write the definition of each part under the flaps. (radius: line segment with endpoints at the center and on the circle; center: the absolute middle of a circle; diameter: line segment with endpoints on the circle that passes through the center; circumference: the distance around the outside of a circle)

5. Cut out the circle and glue it beside the flap book. Then, label the radius, diameter, and center of the circle.

6. Cut out the star. Glue it to the bottom left of the page and complete the formula (circumference = π**d** or 2π**r**).

7. Cut out the three measurement flap books. Cut on the solid lines to create five flaps on the radius and diameter pieces. Apply glue to the gray glue sections and place all three pieces on top of each other to create a stacked flap book with the *Circle Measurements* piece on top. Glue it to the bottom of the page.

8. Complete the flap book using the formulas from the star.

Reflect on Learning

To complete the left-hand page, have students find and measure three circles in the classroom. Then, students should find the circumference of each circle. Students should draw representations of each of their selected circles and record their measurements and calculations.

Answer Key
From top: d = 20, C = 62.8; r = 1, C = 6.3; r = 2.5, d = 5; r = 4.5, d = 9; r = 4, C = 25.1

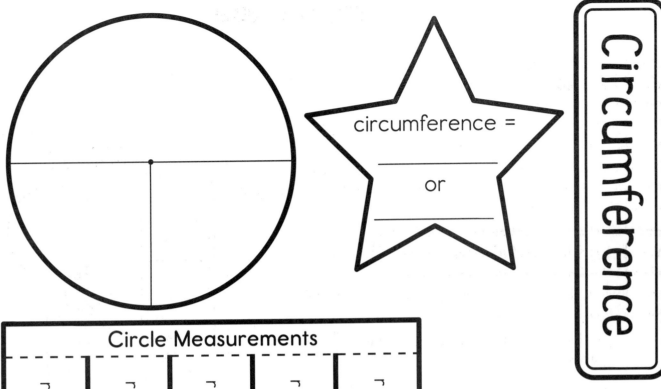

circumference =

_____

or

_____

Circle Measurements

r = ____ yd.	r = ____ in.	r = ____ cm	r = ____ m	r = 10 ft.
glue				
d = 8 yd.	d = ____ in.	d = ____ cm	d = 2 m	d = ____ ft.
glue				
C = ____ yd.	C = 28.3 in.	C = 15.7 cm	C = ____ m	C = ____ ft.

Parts of a Circle

radius

center

diameter

circumference

Area of Circles

Introduction

Draw a 5 x 5 square on the board. Have students work independently to determine the area of the square. Then, call on a volunteer to approach the board and demonstrate how to find the area of the square. As a class, check the students' work. Encourage students to use this information to explain area.

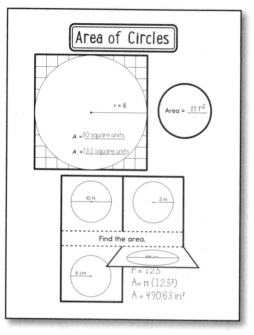

Creating the Notebook Page

Guide students through the following steps to complete the right-hand page in their notebooks.

1. Add a Table of Contents entry for the Area of Circles pages.

2. Cut out the title and glue it to the top of the page.

3. Cut out the circle grid square. Glue it to the top left side of the page.

4. Using the grid as a guide, estimate the area of the circle and write it in the space provided. Discuss the prediction as a class.

5. Cut out the small *Area =* circle and glue it to the top right side of the page.

6. Complete the formula for finding the area of circles (A = πr²). Then, solve to find actual area and write the answer in the space provided. Discuss how the prediction compares to the actual area.

7. Cut out the flap book. Cut on the solid lines to create four flaps. Apply glue to the back of the center section and attach it to the bottom of the page.

8. Calculate the area of each circle and write the answer under the flap.

Reflect on Learning

To complete the left-hand page, have students find three circles around the classroom. Students should take the appropriate measurements and calculate the area of each of their selected circles.

Answer Key
Clockwise from top left: 78.5 ft.²; 28.26 m²; 490.63 in.²; 113 cm²

Area of Circles

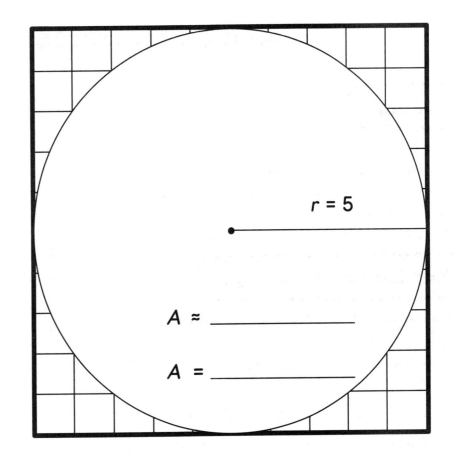

$r = 5$

$A \approx$ _____

$A =$ _____

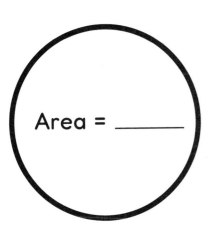

Area = _____

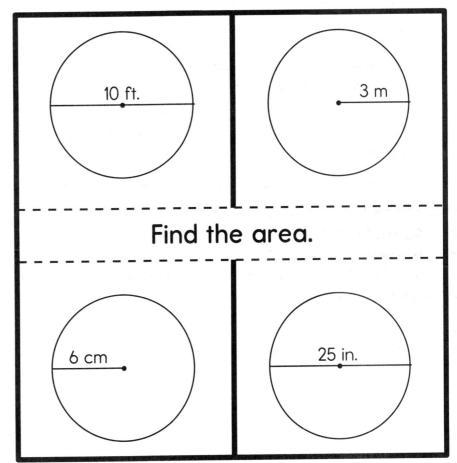

10 ft.

3 m

Find the area.

6 cm

25 in.

Determining Angle Relationships

Introduction

Draw a set of intersecting lines on the board, with the intersection point labeled as *A* and points on each line labeled as *B, C, D, E.* Provide each student with two self-stick notes. Have students write statements about the relationships between the angles on the self-stick notes. The statements can be true or false. Collect and redistribute the completed self-stick notes. Write *True* and *False* on opposite ends of the board. Allow students to place their self-stick notes on the correct side of the board. Discuss each statement.

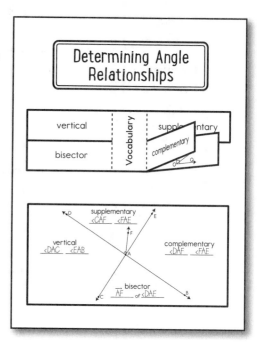

Creating the Notebook Page

Guide students through the following steps to complete the right-hand page in their notebooks.

1. Add a Table of Contents entry for the Determining Angle Relationships pages.

2. Cut out the title and glue it to the top of the page.

3. Cut out the two flap books. Cut on the solid lines to create four flaps on each flap book. Apply glue to the gray glue section and place the *Vocabulary* flap book on top to create a stacked eight-flap book. Apply glue to the back of the center section and attach it to the page below the title.

4. Under the top flaps, highlight the angles that show the relationship described (vertical: ∠*ABD* and ∠*CBE;* bisector: $\overrightarrow{GH}$ and ∠*FGI;* supplementary: ∠*JKL* and ∠*LKM;* complementary: ∠*NOP* and ∠*POQ*). Under each angle flap, explain the relationship. For example, ∠*ABD* and ∠*CBE* are across from each other and are congruent.

5. Cut out the large rectangle and glue it to the bottom of the page.

6. List angles that match each criterion given. Highlight the term to describe each set of angles or segments with a different color. Then, highlight each set of angles or segments with matching colors.

Reflect on Learning

To complete the left-hand page, have students create a set of angles and describe the relationships between them using appropriate vocabulary.

Answer Key

Clockwise from top: Answers will vary but may include ∠*DAE,* ∠*EAB;* ∠*DAF,* ∠*FAE;* $\overrightarrow{AF}$ of ∠*DAE;* ∠*CAD,* ∠*BAE.*

Determining Angle Relationships

vertical	**Vocabulary**	supplementary
bisector		complementary

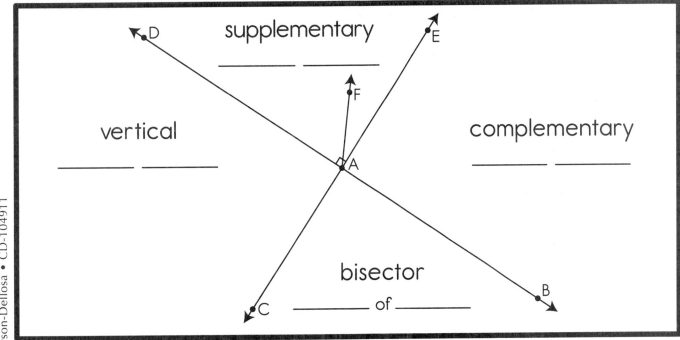

glue

supplementary

_____ _____

vertical

_____ _____

complementary

_____ _____

bisector

_____ of _____

Calculating Angles

Introduction

Review supplementary and complementary angles by passing out index cards that show various types of angle relationships (complementary, supplementary, vertical, and bisectors). Have students identify the types of angle relationships on their cards. Then, ask students to draw sets of angles on the reverse side of their index cards showing different types of angle relationships. Call on volunteers to share and explain their work.

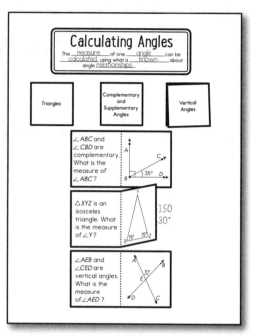

Creating the Notebook Page

Guide students through the following steps to complete the right-hand page in their notebooks.

1. Add a Table of Contents entry for the Calculating Angles pages.

2. Cut out the title and glue it to the top of the page.

3. Complete the explanation. (The **measure** of one **angle** can be **calculated** using what is **known** about angle **relationships**.)

4. Cut out the three accordion fold pieces. For each piece, start with the title section and accordion fold on the dashed lines. Apply glue to the back of each last section. Attach them in a row below the title.

5. Discuss how to use known angles to find unknown angles in each case.

6. Cut out the three flaps. Apply glue to the back of each left section. Attach them in a column below the accordion folds.

7. Calculate the measure of the unknown angle under each flap. Show your work.

Reflect on Learning

To complete the left-hand page, have students create two representations of other types of angle relationships and calculate the unknown angle measures.

58

© Carson-Dellosa • CD-104911

Calculating Angles

The _____ of one _____ can be
_____ using what is _____ about
angle _____.

Solve to find the unknown angle.

Create a subtraction problem using 90° or 180° and the known angle.

∠ABC and ∠CBD are complementary. What is the measure of ∠ABC?

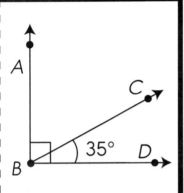

△XYZ is an isosceles triangle. What is the measure of ∠Y?

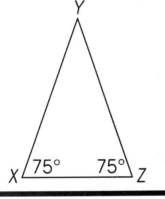

∠AEB and ∠CED are vertical angles. What is the measure of ∠AED?

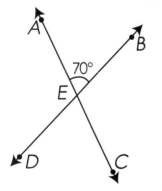

Triangles

Use known angles to subtract and find the unknown angle.

The sum of the angles in a triangle is 180°.

Vertical Angles

Use known angles to find unknown angles.

A pair of intersecting lines creates vertical and supplementary angles.

Sampling

Introduction

Have students line up from tallest to shortest. Record each student's height on the board. Tell students that this data is a sample of the height of seventh graders at the school. Then, split the class in half at the middle of the line and collect only the heights of the tallest half. Point out that the new sample only includes students who are on the taller side. As a class, discuss why it would be problematic to use the second sample.

Creating the Notebook Page

Guide students through the following steps to complete the right-hand page in their notebooks.

1. Add a Table of Contents entry for the Sampling pages.

2. Cut out the title and glue it to the top of the page.

3. Cut out the *Vocabulary* flap book. Cut on the solid lines to create three flaps. Apply glue to the back of the top section and attach it below the title.

4. Cut out the three definition pieces and glue each one under the correct flap. (Biased Data: data that is collected in a way that shows a particular outcome; Random Data: data that is collected randomly and represents a population; Outlier: a piece of data that is significantly different from the rest of the data set)

5. Cut out the *Examples* flap book. Cut on the solid lines to create three flaps. Apply glue to the back of the left section and attach it to the bottom of the page.

6. Cut out the example pieces. Read each example and glue it under the correct flap.

Reflect on Learning

To complete the left-hand page, have students think of and explain a type of data set they could collect. Students should describe how they might collect a random sample, a biased sample, and an outlier.

Vocabulary

Biased Data	Random Data	Outlier

data that is collected in a way that shows a particular outcome

data that is collected randomly and represents a population

a piece of data that is significantly different from the rest of the data set

Examples

Biased Data

Random Data

Outlier

A car company sends a survey to only their customers to see which type of car they prefer.

A mall surveys every fifth person leaving the mall about their experience.

One computer used for a speed test was much older than the others.

Out of all seventh graders, only one student has visited 10 different countries.

The principal asks only students in the eighth-grade hallway what the new lunch entrée should be.

The school randomly selects 300 students to ask them if they use their lockers daily.

Drawing Inferences

Introduction

Draw a Venn diagram on the board. Label one circle *Drawing Inferences in Reading* and one circle *Drawing Inferences in Math*. Have students create their own Venn diagrams with partners and discuss what they think is similar and different about drawing inferences in each subject area. Then, discuss the groups' findings as a class while completing the Venn diagram on the board.

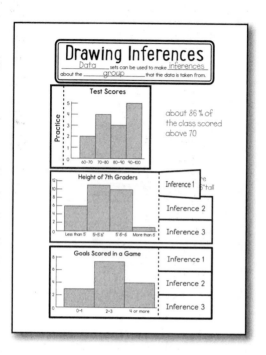

Creating the Notebook Page

Guide students through the following steps to complete the right-hand page in their notebooks.

1. Add a Table of Contents entry for the Drawing Inferences pages.

2. Cut out the title and glue it to the top of the page.

3. Complete the explanation. (**Data** sets can be used to make **inferences** about the **group** that the data is taken from.)

4. Cut out the *Practice* flap. Apply glue to the back of the left section and attach it to the left side of the page below the title.

5. Cut out the fill-in-the-blank rectangle and glue it under the *Practice* flap.

6. Complete the inferences. (1. **3** students scored between **80** and 90. 2. There are **14** students in the class. 3. **50%** of the class scored between 70 and **90**.) Create a fourth inference based on the data and write it on the page to the right of the histogram.

8. Cut out the two flap books. Cut on the solid lines to create three flaps on each one. Then, apply glue to the back of each left section and attach it to the bottom of the page.

9. Use the data to create three inferences for each data set. Write one inference under each flap.

Reflect on Learning

To complete the left-hand page, have students collect a specific type of data from their classmates. Have them list the data and graph it, if possible. Then, have students write three inferences about the data they collected.

Drawing Inferences

about the _____ sets can be used to make _____ that the data is taken from.

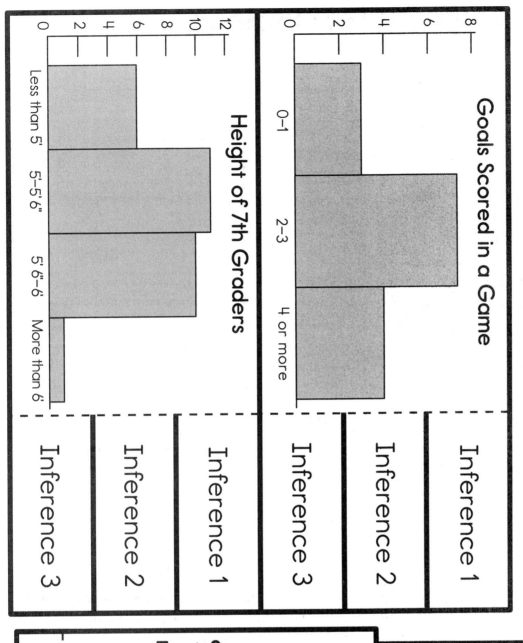

Goals Scored in a Game

0–1
2–3
4 or more

0 2 4 6 8

Height of 7th Graders

Less than 5'
5'–5'6"
5'6"–6'
More than 6'

0 2 4 6 8 10 12

Inference 1
Inference 2
Inference 3

Inference 1
Inference 2
Inference 3

Practice

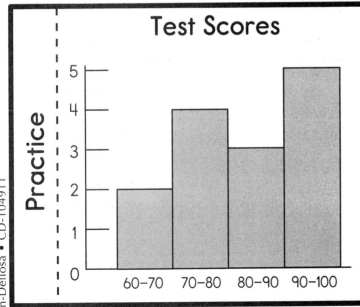

Test Scores

5
4
3
2
1
0

60–70   70–80   80–90   90–100

1. _____ students scored between _____ and 90.

2. There are _____ students in the class.

3. _____ % of the class scored between 70 and _____ .

Measures of Center and Variability

Introduction

Write the data set *2, 3, 4, 5, 5, 6, 8* on the board. Have students work with partners to determine various ways they could summarize the data set. Discuss as a class.

Creating the Notebook Page

Guide students through the following steps to complete the right-hand page in their notebooks.

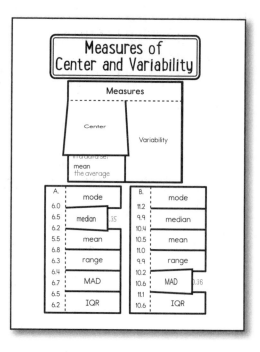

1. Add a Table of Contents entry for the Measures of Center and Variability pages.

2. Cut out the title and glue it to the top of the page.

3. Cut out the two-flap flap books. Cut on the solid line to create two flaps. Apply glue to the gray glue section and place the *Measures* flap book on top to create a stacked flap book. Glue to it to the page below the title.

4. Under the top flaps, write the meanings of the listed terms.

5. Cut out the six-flap flap books. Cut on the solid lines to create six flaps on each. Apply glue to the back of the left section of each flap book and attach them side by side on the bottom of the page.

6. Find each measure of center and measure of variability for each data set listed. Write the answers under each flap.

Reflect on Learning

To complete the left-hand page, have students explain how measures of center and variability can be used to draw additional inferences about data sets. Students should make one inference about each of the data sets listed based on the measures of center and variability.

Answer Key
Data set A: mode: 6.2, 6.5; median: 6.35; mean: 6.31; range: 1.3; MAD: 0.27; IQR: 0.3; Data set B: mode: 9.9, 10.6; median: 10.55; mean: 10.54; range: 1.3; MAD: 0.36; IQR: 0.8

Measures

Variability

Center

glue

range

mean absolute deviation (MAD)

interquartile range (IQR)

mode

median

mean

Measures of Center and Variability

A.		B.	
	mode		mode
6.0		11.2	
6.5	median	9.9	median
6.2		10.4	
5.5	mean	10.5	mean
6.8		11.0	
6.3	range	9.9	range
6.4		10.2	
6.7	MAD	10.6	MAD
6.5		11.1	
6.2	IQR	10.6	IQR

Comparing Data Sets

Provide the following scenario to students: *Students collected the heights of sixth graders and seventh graders. The average height of sixth graders was 49 inches and the average height of seventh graders was 52 inches. The range of the height of sixth graders was 12 inches and the range of the height of seventh graders was 13 inches.* Have students discuss what comparisons they can make between sixth graders' and seventh graders' height using this information.

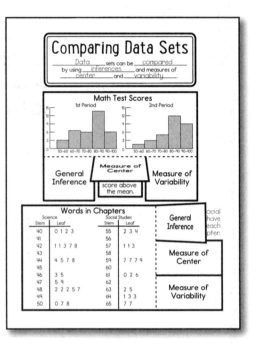

Creating the Notebook Page

Guide students through the following steps to complete the right-hand page in their notebooks.

1. Add a Table of Contents entry for the Comparing Data Sets pages.

2. Cut out the title and glue it to the top of the page.

3. Complete the explanation. (**Data** sets can be **compared** by using **inferences** and measures of **center** and **variability**.) Discuss what it means to make a comparison based on a general inference, a measure of center, and a measure of variability.

4. Cut out the *Math Test Scores* flap book. Cut on the solid lines to create three flaps. Apply glue to the back of the top section and attach it below the title.

5. Cut out the three small rectangles. Glue each one under the appropriate flap. (General Inference: Second period has fewer students. Measure of Center: Second period had more students score above the mean. Measure of Variability: About one-sixth of each class scored between 70 and 80.)

6. Cut out the *Words in Chapters* flap book. Cut on the solid lines to create three flaps. Apply glue to the back of the left section and attach it to the bottom of the page.

7. Make one inference for each category listed on the flaps. Write each inference under the appropriate flap.

Reflect on Learning

To complete the left-hand page, have students partner to collect data from their classmates on a question of their interest. Students should split the data into two sets in any way they choose (e.g., gender, interests, etc.). Then, students should make two or three comparisons between the two data sets.

Comparing Data Sets

_____ sets can be _____ by using _____ and measures of _____ and _____.

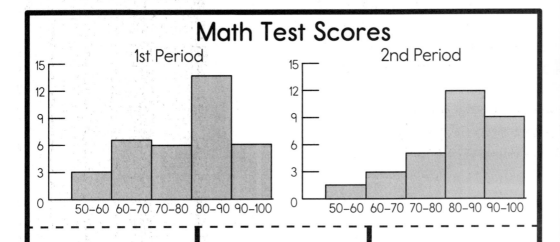

Math Test Scores

1st Period

2nd Period

One-sixth of each class scored between 70 and 80.

Second period had more students score above the mean.

Second period has fewer students.

General Inference	Measure of Center	Measure of Variability

Words in Chapters

Science		Social Studies	
Stem	Leaf	Stem	Leaf
40	0 1 2 3	55	2 3 4
41		56	
42	1 1 3 7 8	57	1 1 3
43		58	
44	4 5 7 8	59	7 7 7 9
45		60	
46	3 5	61	0 2 6
47	5 9	62	
48	2 2 2 5 7	63	2 5
49		64	1 3 3
50	0 7 8	65	7 7

General Inference

Measure of Center

Measure of Variability

Understanding Probability

Introduction

Show students a standard die. Ask students how many sides are on the die (6). Ask students how many different numbers are possible when you roll one standard die (6). Explain that the numbers are outcomes and that the likelihood that you will roll any one specific number is probability.

Creating the Notebook Page

Guide students through the following steps to complete the right-hand page in their notebooks.

1. Add a Table of Contents entry for the Understanding Probability pages.

2. Cut out the title and glue it to the top of the page.

3. Cut out the flap book. Cut on the solid lines to create six flaps on each side. Apply glue to the back of the center section and attach it to the page.

4. Write the definition of each term under the flap on the left side. (probability: a number telling the likelihood that a particular result will occur; outcome: a possible result of an event; certain: will definitely happen; likely: will probably happen; unlikely: will probably not happen; impossible: cannot occur) Write an example of each term under the flap on the right side.

5. Discuss how probability is always given as a number between 0 and 1. Relate it to weather predictions. Look at the number line on the flap book and label the correct ends with 0 (impossible), and 1 (certain). Label $\frac{1}{2}$ and discuss what fractions could represent the terms *likely* and *unlikely*.

Reflect on Learning

To complete the left-hand page, have students sort the words *probability, outcome, certain, likely, unlikely,* and *impossible* into three categories based on their meanings. Students should explain why they categorized the words the way they did.

Understanding Probability		
definition	probability	example
definition	outcome	example
definition	certain	example
definition	likely	example
definition	unlikely	example
definition	impossible	example

Understanding Probability

definition	**probability**	example
definition	**outcome**	example
definition	**certain**	example
definition	**likely**	example
definition	**unlikely**	example
definition	**impossible**	example

Theoretical and Experimental Probability

Students will need a sharpened pencil and a paper clip in order to complete the spinner activity.

Introduction

Show students one die. Ask students to list the possible outcomes when the die is rolled. After finding the number of possible outcomes, have students work with partners to decide what the chance is of rolling a 1 each time the die is rolled.

Creating the Notebook Page

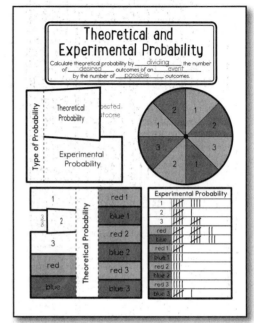

Guide students through the following steps to complete the right-hand page in their notebooks.

1. Add a Table of Contents entry for the Theoretical and Experimental Probability pages.

2. Cut out the title and glue it to the top of the page.

3. Complete the explanation. (Calculate theoretical probability by **dividing** the number of **desired** outcomes of an **event** by the number of **possible** outcomes.)

4. Cut out the *Type of Probability* flap book. Cut on the solid line to create two flaps. Apply glue to the back of the left section and attach it to the left side of the page below the title. Then, discuss the difference between theoretical and experimental probability and define each under the flap. (theoretical: the expected outcome; experimental: the actual outcome)

5. Cut out the spinner and glue it to the right side of the page below the title. Color the spinner red and blue. Begin with red on the top right 1 and alternate colors around the circle.

6. Cut out the *Theoretical Probability* flap book. Cut on the solid lines to create five or six flaps on each side. Apply glue to the back of the center section and attach it to the bottom left of the page. Color each flap red or blue as indicated on the flap.

7. Calculate the theoretical probability of each outcome and write it under the appropriate flap. (1: $\frac{3}{8}$; 2: $\frac{3}{8}$; 3: $\frac{1}{4}$; red: $\frac{1}{2}$; blue: $\frac{1}{2}$; red 1: $\frac{1}{4}$; blue 1: $\frac{1}{8}$; red 2: $\frac{1}{8}$; blue 2: $\frac{1}{4}$; red 3: $\frac{1}{8}$; blue 3: $\frac{1}{8}$)

8. Cut out the *Experimental Probability* chart. Glue it to the bottom right of the page.

9. Use a sharpened pencil and paper clip to spin the spinner at least 25 times. Make a tally mark for each time you spin the outcomes listed.

Reflect on Learning

To complete the left-hand page, have students write two to three sentences comparing the results of their experimental probability experiment with the theoretical probabilities they calculated.

Theoretical and Experimental Probability

Calculate theoretical probability by _____ the number of _____ outcomes of an _____ by the number of _____ outcomes.

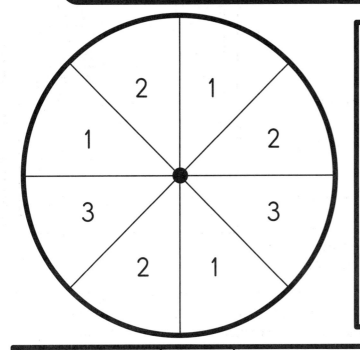

Type of Probability	Theoretical Probability
	Experimental Probability

Theoretical Probability		
1		red 1
2		blue 1
3		red 2
		blue 2
red		red 3
blue		blue 3

Experimental Probability	
1	
2	
3	
red	
blue	
red 1	
blue 1	
red 2	
blue 2	
red 3	
blue 3	

Uniform Probability Models

Introduction

Place five different items in a bag. Show students the items as they are placed in the bag. Then, begin pulling items from the bag. Ask students to name the probability of pulling that item out of the bag. Each time, write the probability on the board (⅕) and then replace the items in the bag. Repeat several times. Compare the possibility of pulling each item, and discuss why it was the same for every item.

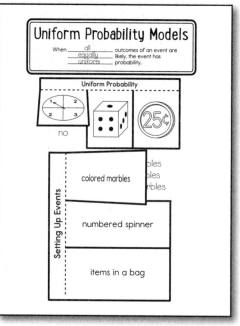

Creating the Notebook Page

Guide students through the following steps to complete the right-hand page in their notebooks.

1. Add a Table of Contents entry for the Uniform Probability Models pages.

2. Cut out the title and glue it to the top of the page.

3. Complete the explanation. (When **all** outcomes of an event are **equally** likely, the event has **uniform** probability.)

4. Cut out the *Uniform Probability* flap book. Cut on the solid lines to create three flaps. Apply glue to the back of the top section and attach it to the page below the title.

5. Under each flap, write *yes* or *no* to indicate whether the scenario has uniform probability. Tell students to assume that the die is a standard die and that the coin is a standard coin.

6. Cut out the *Setting Up Events* flap book. Cut on the solid lines to create three flaps. Apply glue to the back of the left section and attach it to the bottom of the page.

7. Under each flap describe and illustrate an event with uniform probability.

Reflect on Learning

To complete the left-hand page, have students write about three scenarios in which having a uniform probability of an outcome would be important.

Uniform Probability Models

When _____ outcomes of an event are _____ likely, the event has _____ probability.

Setting Up Events

colored marbles

numbered spinner

items in a bag

Uniform Probability

Probability Models

Introduction

Draw a spinner on the board that is split into eight equal sections. Use four different colors to shade the sections of the spinner (four sections one color, two sections a second color, and the remaining two sections a final color). Have students work with partners to answer the following questions: Which color is most likely to be landed on? Which colors are equally likely to be landed on? What is the probability of spinning ____?

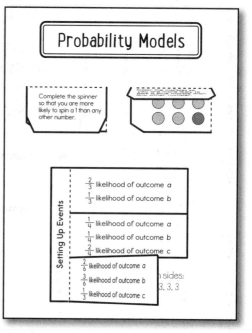

Creating the Notebook Page

Guide students through the following steps to complete the right-hand page in their notebooks.

1. Add a Table of Contents entry for the Probability Models pages.

2. Cut out the title and glue it to the top of the page.

3. Cut out the two L-shaped pieces. Place each piece with the text face down and fold in the side with the drawing. Then, fold down the top flap. Apply glue to the gray glue sections and attach them side by side on the top of the page.

4. On each picture flap, draw the situation described. Then, create the same probability by drawing a different version of the same model on the inside of each flap book. For example, on the spinner flap book, draw a spinner that has six equal spaces but is still more likely to spin a 1.

5. Cut out the *Setting Up Events* flap book. Cut on the solid lines to create three flaps. Apply glue to the back of the left section and attach it to the bottom of the page.

6. Under each flap, describe and illustrate an event to match the outcomes described under each flap.

Reflect on Learning

To complete the left-hand page, have students write about why understanding probability is important in real life. Have students include one example describing when they would need to use probability.

glue

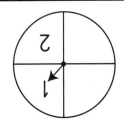

Complete the spinner so that you are more likely to spin a 1 than any other number.

Color the marbles so that you are more likely to pick a blue marble than any other color.

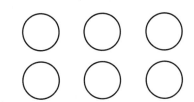

glue

Setting Up Events

$\frac{2}{3}$ likelihood of outcome *a*

$\frac{1}{3}$ likelihood of outcome *b*

$\frac{1}{4}$ likelihood of outcome *a*

$\frac{1}{4}$ likelihood of outcome *b*

$\frac{2}{4}$ likelihood of outcome *c*

$\frac{2}{6}$ likelihood of outcome *a*

$\frac{3}{6}$ likelihood of outcome *b*

$\frac{1}{3}$ likelihood of outcome *c*

Compound Events

Introduction

Draw an equally-divided four-section spinner on the board with each section labeled with a different number. Draw three circles on the board colored three different colors to represent marbles. Have students discuss the number of possible outcomes when the spinner is spun. Then, have students discuss the number of possible outcomes when a marble is selected. Finally, discuss what might happen when the spinner and marbles are used together to create an event.

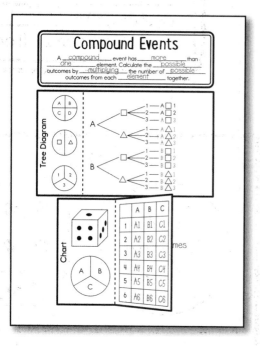

Creating the Notebook Page

Guide students through the following steps to complete the right-hand page in their notebooks.

1. Add a Table of Contents entry for the Compound Events pages.

2. Cut out the title and glue it to the top of the page.

3. Complete the explanation. (A **compound** event has **more** than **one** element. Calculate the **possible** outcomes by **multiplying** the number of **possible** outcomes from each **element** together.)

4. Cut out the *Tree Diagram* flap. Apply glue to the back of the left section and attach it to the bottom of the page.

5. Complete the tree diagram on the flap based on the spinners. Draw the rest of the tree under the flap. Write the number of possible outcomes under the flap. Confirm the number of possible outcomes using the multiplication method.

6. Cut out the *Chart* rectangle. Apply glue to the back of the left section and attach it to the bottom of the page.

7. Complete the chart on the flap based on the die and spinner. Write the number of possible outcomes under the flap using the multiplication method.

Reflect on Learning

To complete the left-hand page, have students design their own compound events. They should show all of the possible outcomes of the events.

Compound Events

A _____ event has _____ than _____ element. Calculate the _____ outcomes by _____ the number of _____ outcomes from each _____ together.

Chart

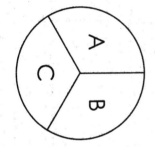 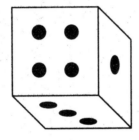

	A	B	C
1			
2			
3			
4			
5			
6			

Tree Diagram

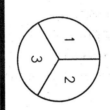 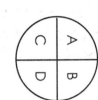

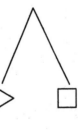

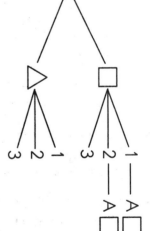

Tabs

Cut out each tab and label it. Apply glue to the back of each tab and align it on the outside edge of the page with only the label section showing beyond the edge. Then, fold each tab to seal the page inside.

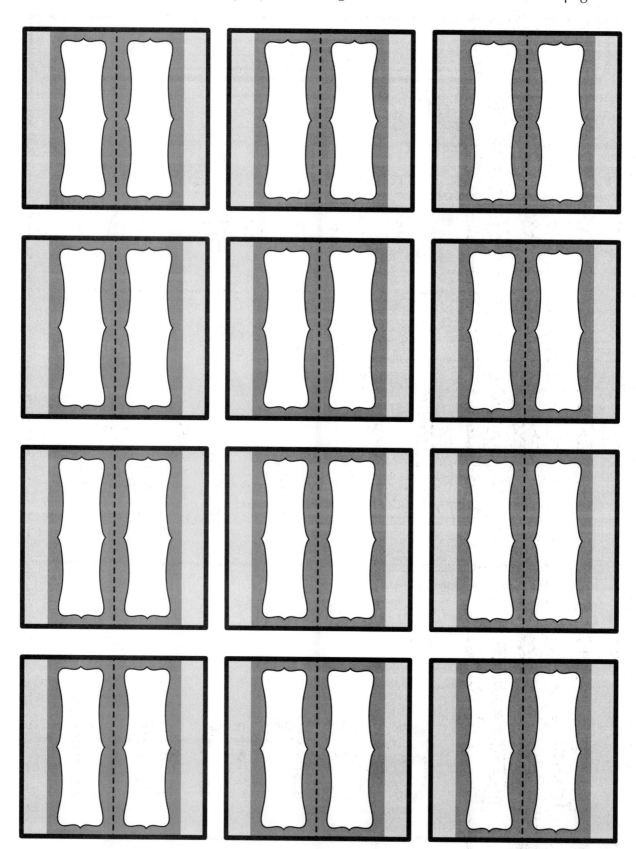

Cut out the KWL chart and cut on the solid lines to create three separate flaps. Apply glue to the back of the Topic section to attach the chart to a notebook page.

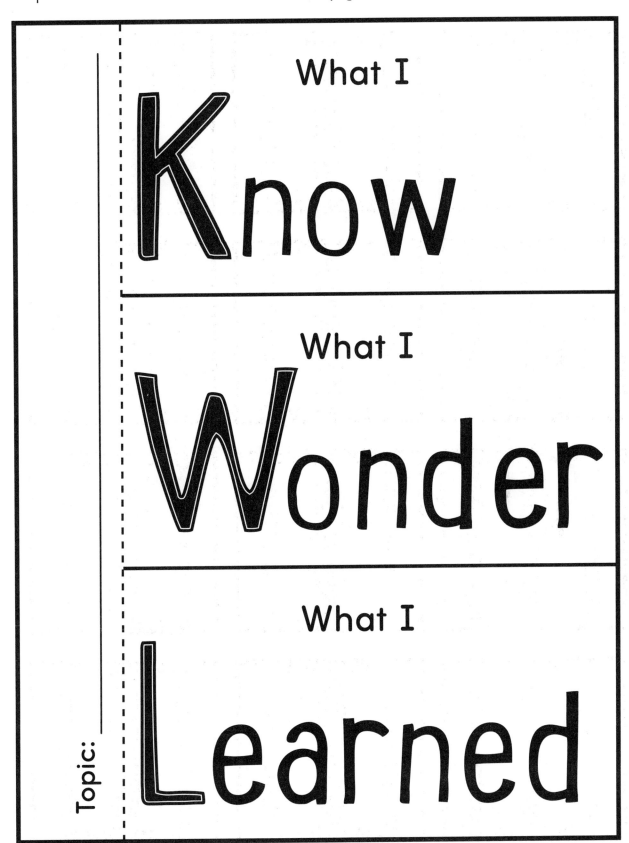

Library Pocket

Cut out the library pocket on the solid lines. Fold in the side tabs and apply glue to them before folding up the front of the pocket. Apply glue to the back of the pocket to attach it to a notebook page.

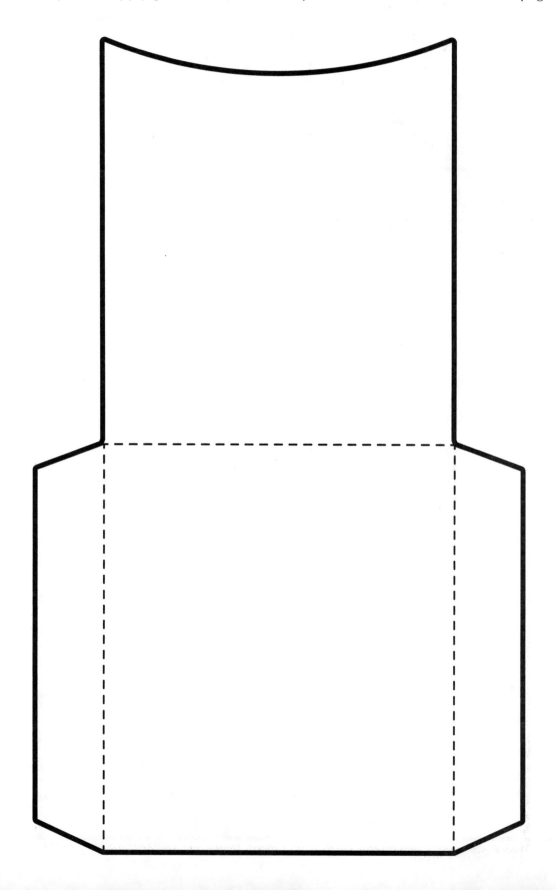

Envelope

Cut out the envelope on the solid lines. Fold in the side tabs and apply glue to them before folding up the rectangular front of the envelope. Fold down the triangular flap to close the envelope. Apply glue to the back of the envelope to attach it to a notebook page.

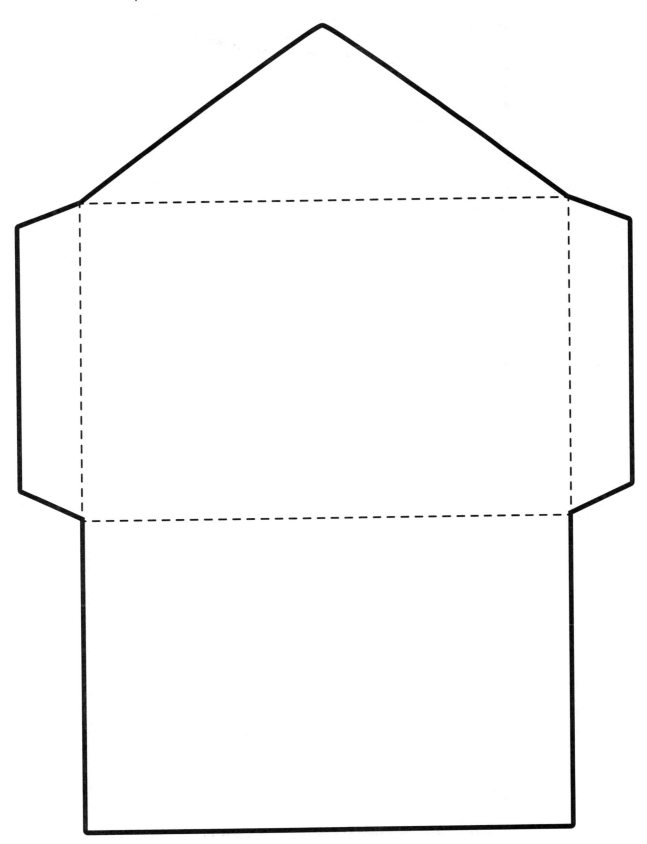

Pocket and Cards

Cut out the pocket on the solid lines. Fold over the front of the pocket. Then, apply glue to the tabs and fold them around the back of the pocket. Apply glue to the back of the pocket to attach it to a notebook page. Cut out the cards and store them in the envelope.

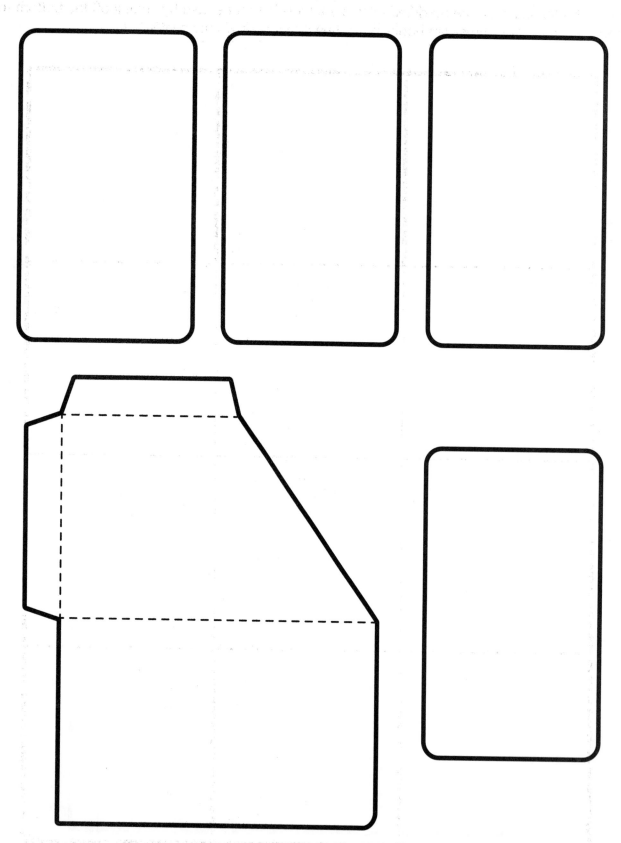

Six-Flap Shutter Fold

Cut out the shutter fold around the outside border. Then, cut on the solid lines to create six flaps. Fold the flaps toward the center. Apply glue to the back of the shutter fold to attach it to a notebook page.

If desired, this template can be modified to create a four-flap shutter fold by cutting off the bottom row. You can also create two three-flap books by cutting it in half down the center line.

Eight-Flap Shutter Fold

Cut out the shutter fold around the outside border. Then, cut on the solid lines to create eight flaps. Fold the flaps toward the center. Apply glue to the back of the shutter fold to attach it to a notebook page.

If desired, this template can be modified to create two four-flap shutter folds by cutting off the bottom two rows. You can also create two four-flap books by cutting it in half down the center line.

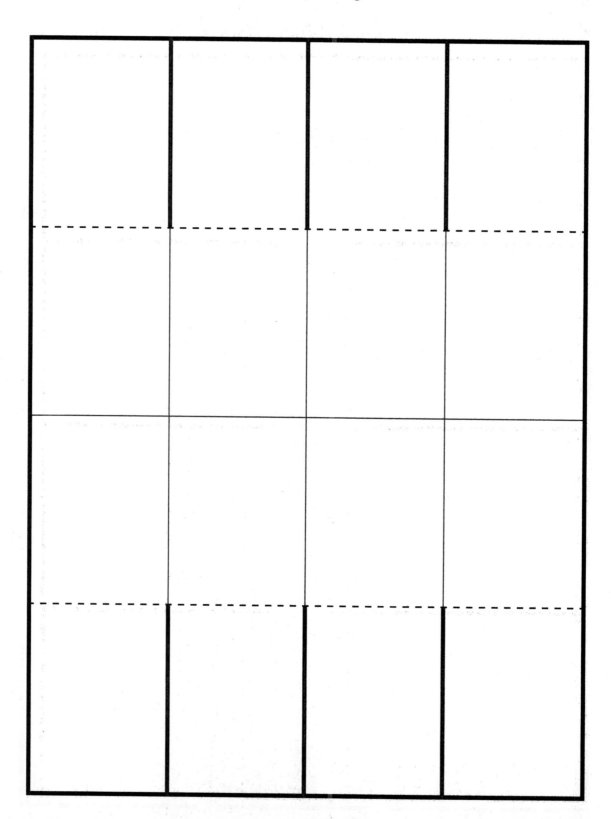

Flap Book—Eight Flaps

Cut out the flap book around the outside border. Then, cut on the solid lines to create eight flaps. Apply glue to the back of the center section to attach it to a notebook page.

If desired, this template can be modified to create a six-flap or two four-flap books by cutting off the bottom row or two. You can also create a tall four-flap book by cutting off the flaps on the left side.

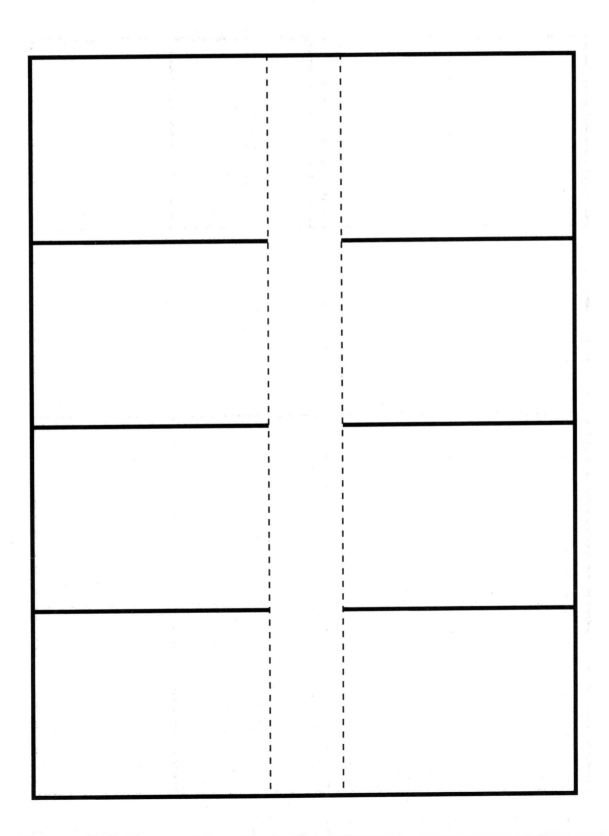

Flap Book—Twelve Flaps

Cut out the flap book around the outside border. Then, cut on the solid lines to create 12 flaps. Apply glue to the back of the center section to attach it to a notebook page.

If desired, this template can be modified to create smaller flap books by cutting off any number of rows from the bottom. You can also create a tall flap book by cutting off the flaps on the left side.

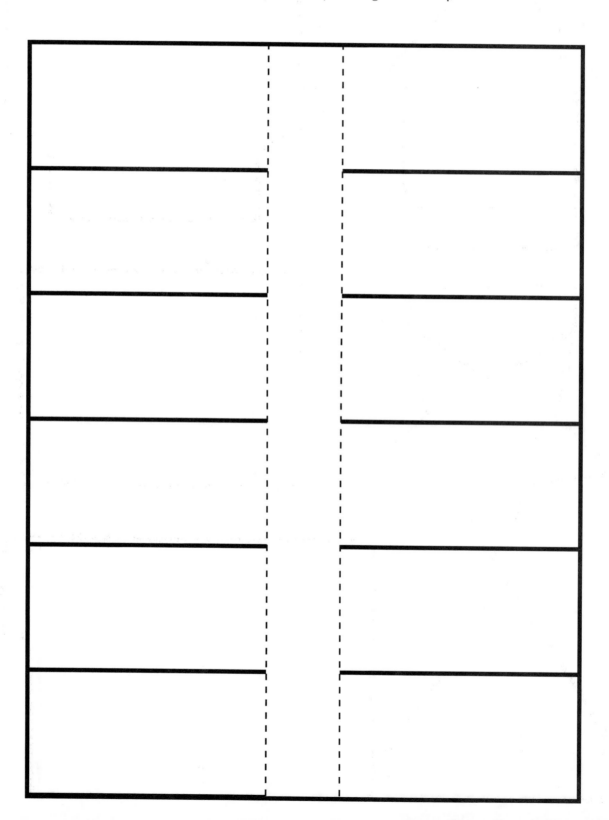

Shaped Flaps

Cut out each shaped flap. Apply glue to the back of the narrow section to attach it to a notebook page.

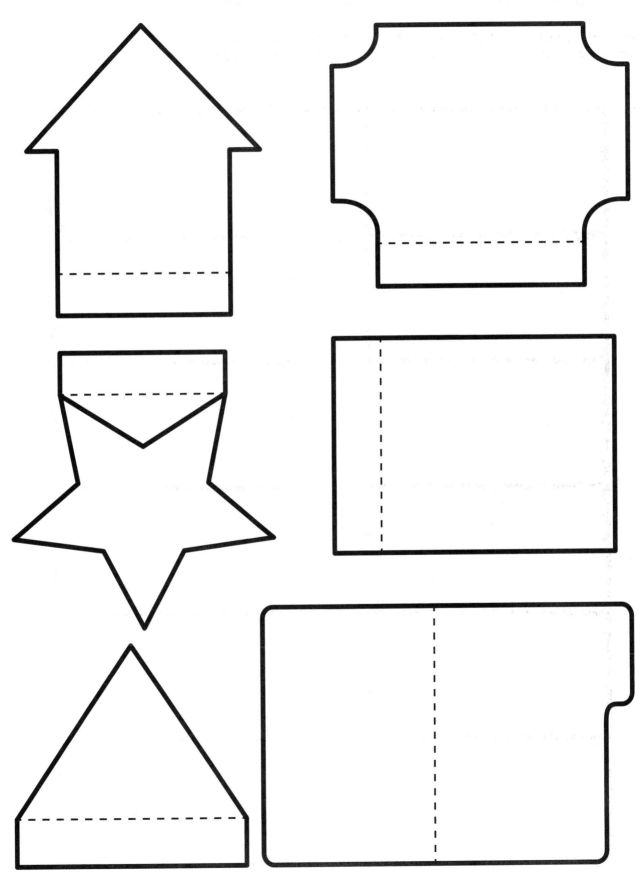

Shaped Flaps

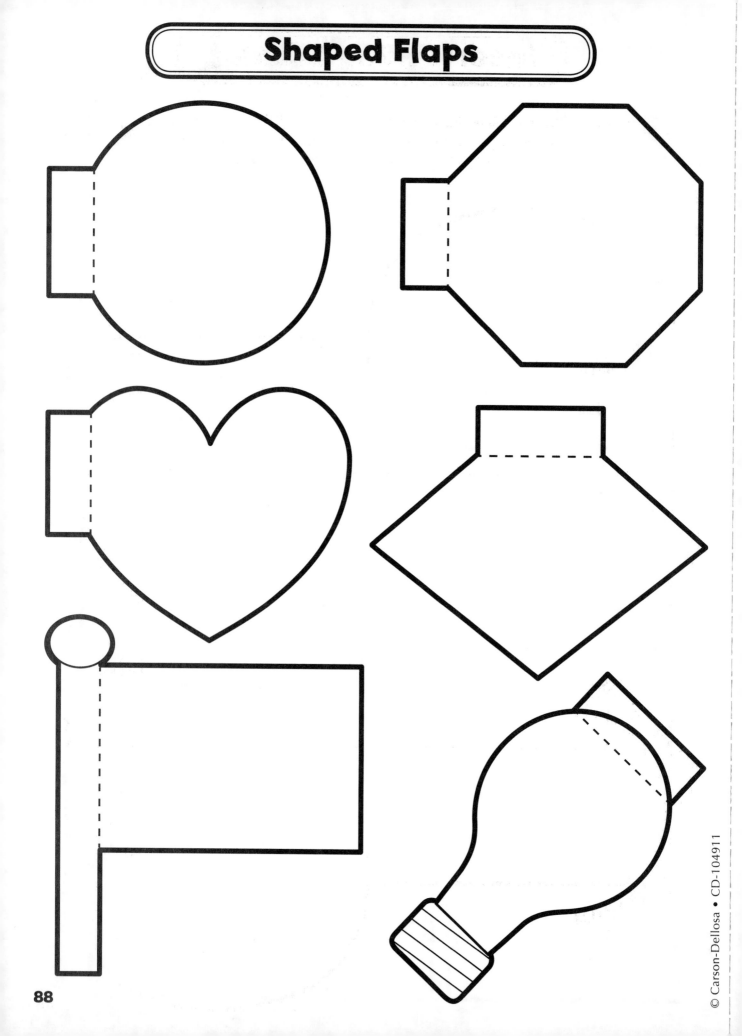

Interlocking Booklet

Cut out the booklet on the solid lines, including the short vertical lines on the top and bottom flaps. Then, fold the top and bottom flaps toward the center, interlocking them using the small vertical cuts. Apply glue to the back of the center panel to attach it to a notebook page.

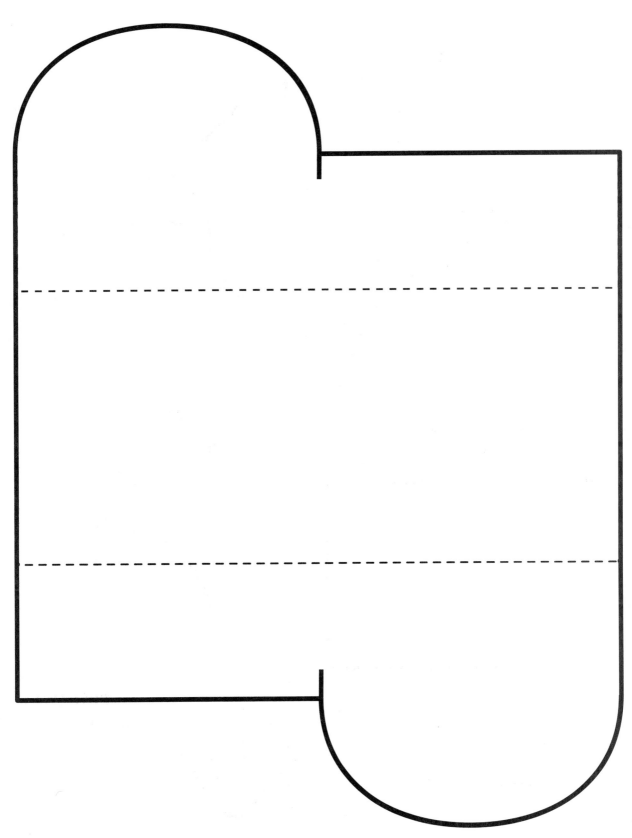

Four-Flap Petal Fold

Cut out the shape on the solid lines. Then, fold the flaps toward the center. Apply glue to the back of the center panel to attach it to a notebook page.

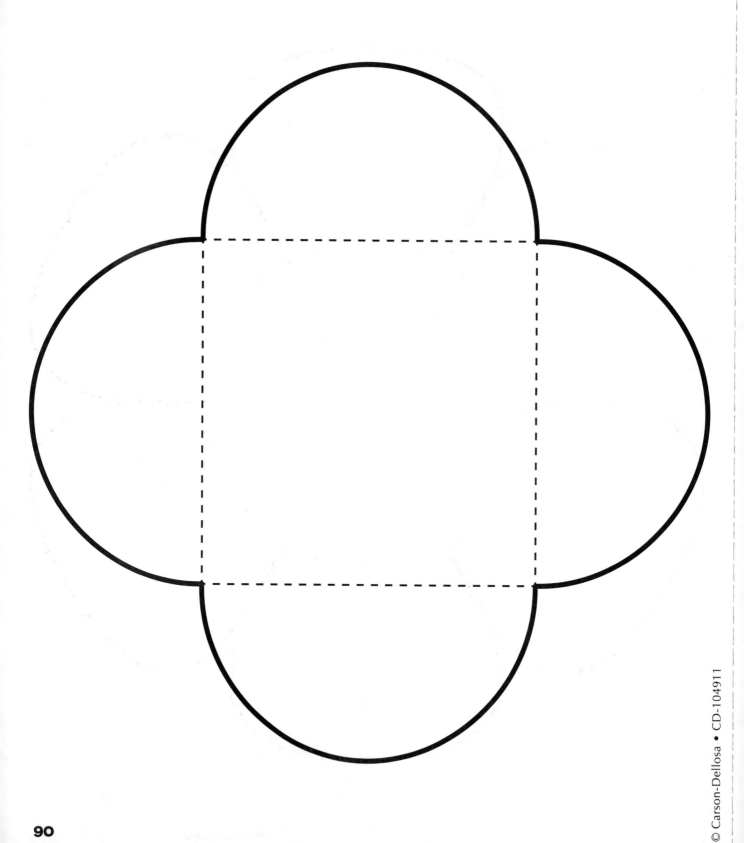

Six-Flap Petal Fold

Cut out the shape on the solid lines. Then, fold the flaps toward the center and back out. Apply glue to the back of the center panel to attach it to a notebook page.

Accordion Folds

Cut out the accordion pieces on the solid lines. Fold on the dashed lines, alternating the fold direction. Apply glue to the back of the last section to attach it to a notebook page.

You may modify the accordion books to have more or fewer pages by cutting off extra pages or by having students glue the first and last panels of two accordion books together.

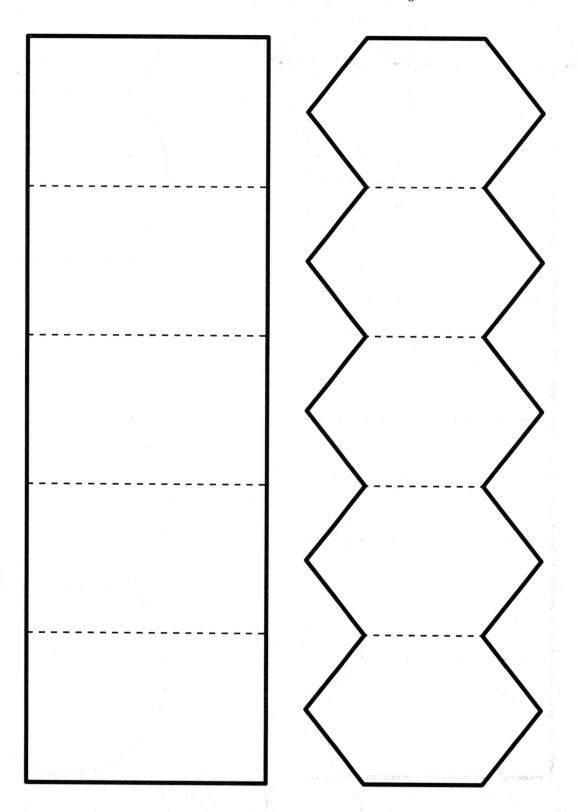

Accordion Folds

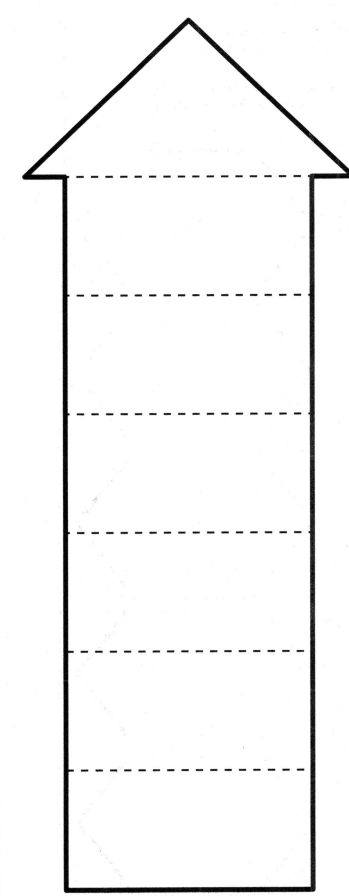

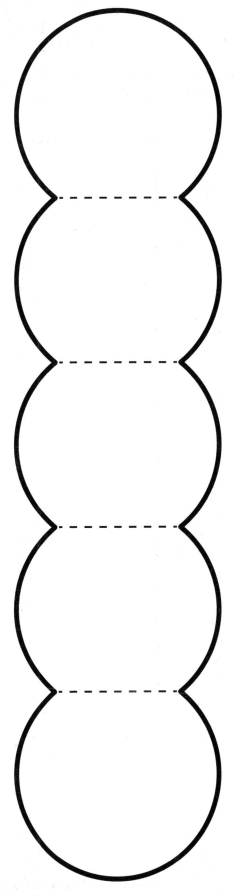

Clamshell Fold

Cut out the clamshell fold on the solid lines. Fold and unfold the piece on the three dashed lines. With the piece oriented so that the folds form an X with a horizontal line through it, pull the left and right sides together at the fold line. Then, keeping the sides touching, bring the top edge down to meet the bottom edge. You should be left with a triangular shape that unfolds into a square. Apply glue to the back of the triangle to attach the clamshell to a notebook page.

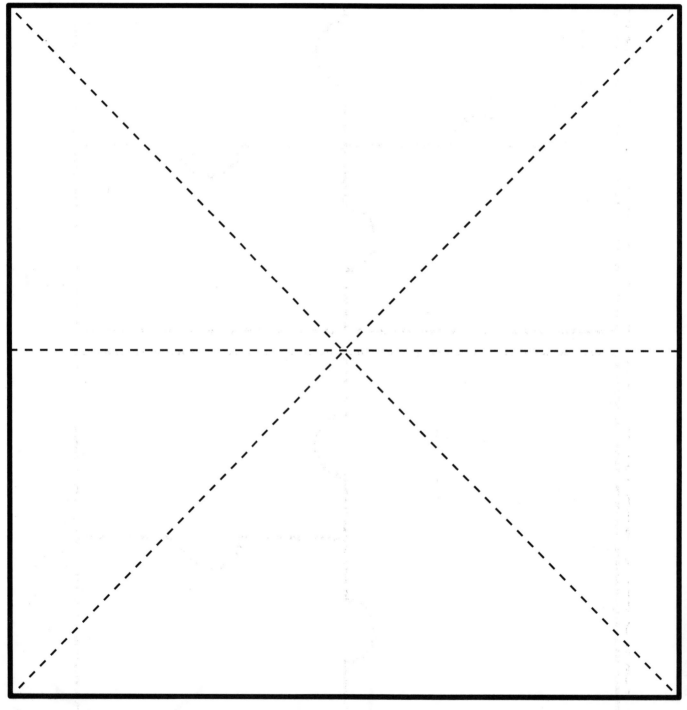

Puzzle Pieces

Cut out each puzzle along the solid lines to create a three- or four-piece puzzle. Apply glue to the back of each puzzle piece to attach it to a notebook page. Alternately, apply glue only to one edge of each piece to create flaps.

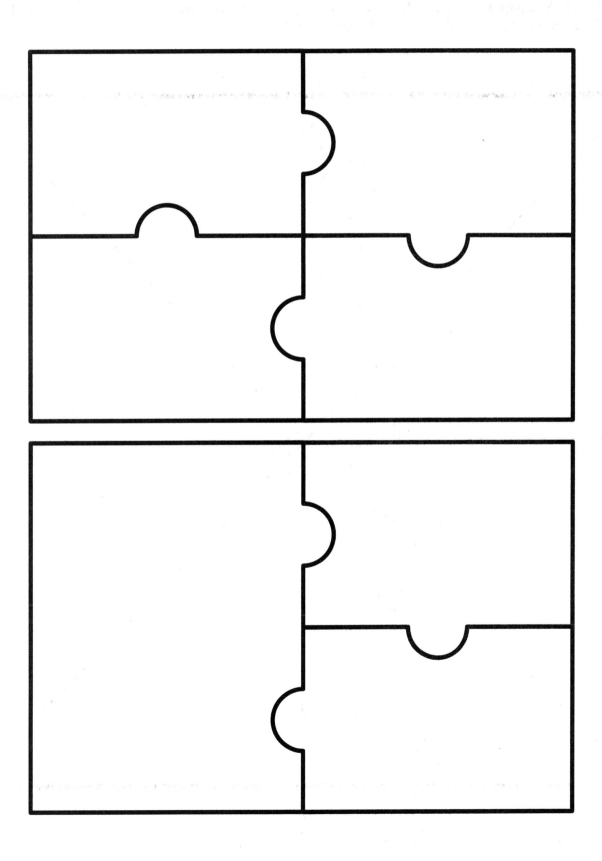

Flip Book

Cut out the two rectangular pieces on the solid lines. Fold each rectangle on the dashed lines. Fold the piece with the gray glue section so that it is inside the fold. Apply glue to the gray glue section and place the other folded rectangle on top so that the folds are nested and create a book with four cascading flaps. Make sure that the inside pages are facing up so that the edges of both pages are visible. Apply glue to the back of the book to attach it to a notebook page.

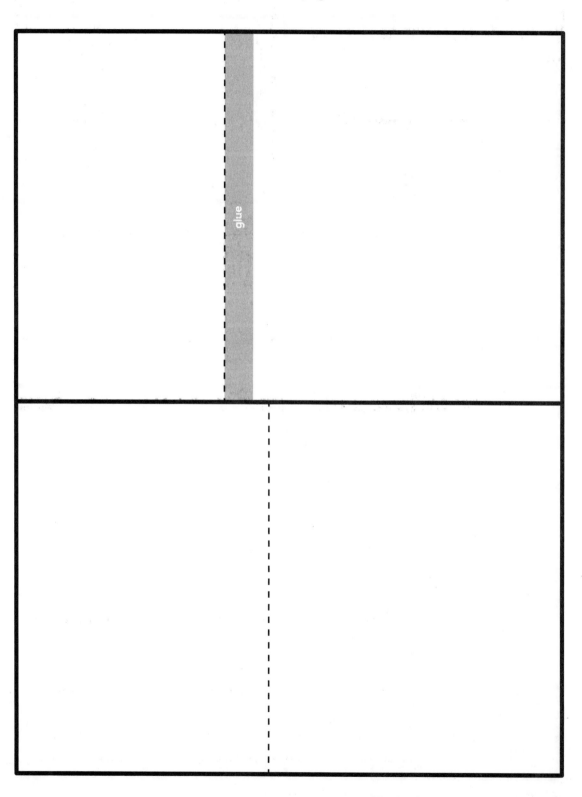

glue